LOVE AND OTHER DANGEROUS DRUGS

Over the years we have all had experiences that have shaped who we are, how we feel, what we think, The very things that shaped our character, and made us into the men and women we are today. Along with societal, community, and family interactions.
The pieces I put together are a look into the things I want, how I feel as a Man, how I see the world, and everything in between.
The thing about putting love on the list with drugs is that love is dangerous.
It can heal you and make you sick. It can take away misery but nothing adds misery like a lonely, broken heart.
In no way am I glorifying drug usage. People make their own decisions. I just say be healthy, and be safe in whatever you choose to do.
This is part story, part frustration release, part showing my talents for writing songs.
This is not something that I just started doing, and there will be more to come.
This is just one key on the chain to the locks of generational wealth and being able to give back and help others in need.
Music has always been a part of my life and writing comes naturally.
This is a way to introduce myself and my skills.
It will speak for itself.

Detonation.
Goin in again, pen hitting the paper, causing another detonation
Blowing up your demonstration, one fell swoop stop all the hateration
Keep a bad bitch, crazy loot, give them bougie bitches the boot
Like them girls if they smoke and drink too
You know who, I Love You
Play the game chess moves, one false move you loose
I see ten moves ahead, I count ten a head
She give me 10 head , then i give her 10 put her to bed
Corn fed but city raised
Chitown snow cold, travel the globe
Feeling like I'm 22 years old
Push it to the limit, red light district
I got a big stick, I would be inappropriate to say dick
But fuck it while we on the subject, girl let melick your clit
Make you cum quick, make your body speak in different languages
Take you to the peak then make you start over again, and again and again

Till the morning light is shining in
I want you for eternity, give you what you want from me
Showing you the very definition of ecstasy
Try me dont deny me I Love You
Detonation all over the nation,
Watch me make waves like a Tsunami, hope you don't think that I don't got no army
Got silent assassins at my beck and call, but they just begging for a chance to end it all
I walk with no fear, No one can harm me here
I got the mind bender, put you in the blender
Better than any suspenseful thriller, until I write it Im that gifted
I could write a thesis on the meaning of life, If I want I can take any woman as my wife
Only see one, the game is over and done
She has claimed my heart and won, Im her moon, she's my sun
Don't worry about how i feel, You Know I Te Amo Nina and that's for real.

A Day Without Love

I've found myself in a place I never wanted to be
All alone with no love, on a day its celebrated universally
Maybe that's what's best for me, learn to love myself unconditionally
Forgive myself for my past mistakes, win my future like a lucky sweepstakes
See a lot of pretty faces, walls with no foundations
Could be a lot of different places
Emotions flowing like gold fountains
Cursed and Blessed with patience
Waiting for a real love that cares for me, so random flings hold no fascination
One I can surrender my heart to, sweep me off my feet, So i can fall deeply
Many of us search for the same thing, lonely hearts that wait for loves ring
If its not sent from above then it doesn't mean a thing
Another day without love, my heart is a useless thing
It beats to keep me alive but i have nothing to feel
No love to keep me grounded, to show me that life is real
No bells and whistles sounded, lonely like the last tree in the field

A Day without Love is an eternity
Searching the skies for a sign still there's no love standing next to me

Walking alone but standing tall, far from home but master of it all
Except for my heart, it does what it wants
Can't tell it when or who to love, sometimes it cuts itself off
Spend a lot of time, dreaming of one to be mine
I can almost see her face, about to teleport to her place

Tired of the endless chase, want a love that can't be replaced
Looking for the one, who makes me feel young
Man, if she's worth it I wouldn't mind being sprung
Love me with no deception, heart as clear as the mirror's reflection
Love is a diamond's physical perfection
Want one that I can adore, push me to the limit, but help me up off the floor
Want her to be my everything, the reason why I write, the reason why I sing
The reason why I went out and bought that diamond ring
The reason why i asked you to change your last name

A Day Without love, is an eternity
Stay searching the skies above, still there's no love standing next to me

Loving someone that doesn't love you back
Is the same as being stabbed with a knife in the back
The pain is intense, no other way to describe it
Heart's in solitary confinement, lost and I can't find it
Love is the cruelest emotion, riding high on its waves
Or drowning in its airless ocean
The sacrifices we make, the daily energy we give and take
The synergy that we create, the bonds that we form and break
Sometimes I think I'm destined to be alone
No special girl, no one to call my own
Wandering through life's journey, mostly all alone

3 Times

Baby, I feel like a marathon tonight, hope you ready

It goes 1, for the hour Imma spend getting your body ready
It goes 2, for the times Imma make you cum
With both my tongue and my body
It goes 3, for the number of times I wanna do it tonight

Baby, oh Baby let's make love 3 times
Baby, oh Baby let's make love 3 times

I wanna see, can you really handle me?
Can you really handle all of this lovin?
I'm going deep, we not gon sleep
The room is as hot as an oven

Put that thang in the air, and imma bury my lovin there,
Baby, oh Baby let's make love 3 times
Baby, oh, Baby

We close to round 3, now you on top of me
You going up and down
#3 different positions, oh baby let me give you what you've been missing
Now we hugging and we kissing

It goes 1 for the hour Imma spend, getting your body ready
It goes 2 for both the times Imma make you cum,
With both my tongue and my body
It goes 3 for the number of times i wanna do it tonight
Baby, oh Baby, let's make love 3 times
Baby, oh Baby let's make love 3 times

A Broken Heart Can make You Become Heartless

I told her that I needed her to be, Heartless
To anyone but Me
I told her that i would be anything she would ever need
I even got down on one bended knee
She turned away and said she didn't feel the same way for me

So now I'm out here heartless
Not trying to feel anything
I'm out here heartless, but I do have my rhymes for company

Nothing inside, no passion, no pride
An empty shell of a man, just going through life's motions
Adrift in humanities ocean
I don't need a gun in my hand, my pen is way more explosive
Sippin on a love potion, waiting for it to kick in
Smoke a blunt to pass, the time, spend a lot of time getting high

Cause I'm out here heartless, not trying to feel anything
Im'm out here heartless, but I do have my rhymes for company

Beautiful ladies smile at me and conversate to pass the time
But anyone who looks at me can see that there is only one on my mind
I try not to think about the pain that I feel, It's too real

Doing the very best I can as a Man
But sometimes it's like my life is a pit of quicksand
I'm reaching out for hands, but there's nobody there to save me
I take solace in the fact that I'm strong cause that's how God Made me

So now I'm out here heartless, Not trying to feel anything
I'm out here heartless but I do have my rhymes for company

BEAST

I need a lioness, that can handle my aggressiveness
Know when to submit, but don't put up with too much of my bullshit
Now I'm rollin legit, she can do a full split
Other shit I do, I don't speak on it
Who you know can travel a mile on foot in under 3 minutes?
I bend time, make it mine
Warp it like a bubble, I see everything like Hubble
I hear her body calling me
I hear everything you say about me
Whether good or bad y'all stay saying my name
Conversations about me, I don't want the fame
But I love the recognition For how I'm killing the game
Like the Witch's Inquisition
Put y'all boys in Salem's lot
Burn em one at a time, like how i smoke my pine
Got diamonds to remind me of the hard times
I shine for a different reason, I shine in every season
I'm a Beast, please believe him
I'm half awake, just let me bake, eat the game like birthday cake
Make a purple diesel protein shake
Make here shake like a mini earthquake
I'm stiff as a board, Fly as a feather, the map is my where ever
I choose to go next, stay strapped like a Nun with a crucifix
None of yall sorry niggas can fuck with this
Eyes like an eagle, strength of a bear
Patience of a hunter, let you walk into my snare
I play the game with honesty,
Gang Gaines, one man army
Rambo style I'm goin in alone
Spittin Beanie Sigel truth shit, sippin 100 prof shit

Bigger Picture

I got the whole perspective, I'm looking at the bigger picture
I'm focused on my inner circle, shield wall
You can't get near a nigga
Always stay thanking God for the figures
Not wasting my time throwing no cash at no strippers
My chick sexy enough, so I don't need to chase ass in no club
I will pop a few bottles in VIP show ya boy some love
Smoke a gang of bud, drink a couple of mugs
Shoot the shit, shoot some pool
Watch a game, act a fool
That's not doing it because of the fame
That's how I've already live my life
Man, wild days at the Spot,shout out to the guys
They used to call me James EvansOr Lil Git Gone
If I was sauced 24/7
Met a bunch of good people, had my own little slice of heaven
But good things come to an end, I done been a whole lot of places
Met a lot of new faces, some good some bad, some happy, some sad
Life is a mixed up grab bag, full of everything under the sun
Whatever you pick, take it, run with it and have fun
Be yourself with no regrets, love yourself with no regrets
Strong as any weapon ever made, they won't prosper
I'm betting on myself like Pete Rose,
In a private, silent chopper
I come through silent like the Phantom Of The Opera
I'm both the irresistible force and the immovable object
There's 2 of me, so what you gonna do with both of me?
One wants to take over Hip-Hop
The other one wants to rule R&B
Gemini, got six eyes,see everything
Know the truth from lies, Angel in disguise

About to change a lot of people's lives
Give em hope when they thought they was about to take they last ride
The world has always been violent, you can see it throughout history
But now it's televised, or spread over the web instantly
Imagine if peace spread just as easily
The world would transform and we could all live equally
No more wars, no more killing, everybody making a living
Parents raising their children

Without the fear of their child going to prison
Or dying for something senseless
I know i can get at least one witness
Six Degrees Of Separation, spread the message to every nation
The Bigger Picture

Candidly Speaking

Smoke weed like I'm at a Pow wow, that's how I been living my life
No longer broke,got a lot of cash now, finally living a better life
Crystal clear vision, spitting with precision
Cutting up the game like incisions, got it jumping like I’m serving pigeons
Smoke a blunt while I’m in a hot air balloon
Go diving off the coast of Cancun, got em tripping like they on shrooms
Got em watching me like old school saturday morning cartoons
Fists of Fury, whoop that ass like Bruce Lee
Judge and jury, execute you in the streets
Just imagine what's gonna happen when i decide to rock a beat
Maybe one day i will make the circle complete
Hitting it straight down the fairway, way out to centerfield
Kick a 66 yard field goal, game winning 3, man Im’m clutch for real
Take a good look at the future, about to take over the planet
Cock of the yard like a rooster, want my girl pretty like young Janet
I want to ball outlandishly, live every night full of revelry
Always going to speak candidly, always dressed impeccably
Nothing but the best next to me
Jimmy Choo on her back, Red Bottoms on her feet
Want to get cash like I’m related to the creator of Mercedes Benz
Damn i’m kind of gone I been smoking on that gas again
Roll Bob Marley joints, I’m sharper than an arrow point
Tighter than a pythons grip, like a Jedi or more like the Glow I got the gift
Trying to get money, plenty amd swift
Make all the ladies want me, the haters can get my middle finger tips
Been to hell and back again, feels like i’ve taken more than one trip
Thank God that I’m not forsaken, my light shines bright through my gift

When goodbye isn't goodbye, it’s until I see you later
The next time, catch you later in the next time
About to leave the planet, smoked too much weed
Now my mind is stranded, feels like my ship just crash landed
Kind of stuck from all the champagne I've been handed
Neck look like I pulled a star down to the planet

Wrist rocky like the iceberg that sank the Titanic
Bull in a china shop, doing a lot of damage
Out in the ocean in Costa Rica, living like a civilized savage
Taking care of my people, love the city that I'm from
No matter how far I go, never forget the city where I was born and raised, Son
CHICAGO W go 6 gold balls, a few Lord Stanley's cups
White Sox got 1, wish the Bears could have repeated in 86
Best game going on the NorthSide of town, my friend
Looking for my Cubs to take that MLB crown again
Lakefront summer nights, young, strong and full of life
Now sometimes I feel colder than Lake Michigan when it's full of ice

Celebration

Oversaturation, I'm rising like inflation
I'm about to take over the nation
Total domination, it's a celebration over here
Yeah, yeah it's a celebration

Got a whole lot of cash now, haters can kiss my ass now
Ball hard like a flagrant foul, got a lot of lil bad chicks by my side now
Stay puffin in the whip, eyes red, I'm high right now
On the way to get another zip, because we don almost ran out
Pretty face, slim waist, keep my baby with a briefcase
Stay stashing shit in the safe, stay on that paper chase
Fly like a pelican, cleaner than the Vatican
Doing it bigger than the Hindenburg
It's the shit you do, it takes way more than words
But I'm pushing these verbs like birds
Ounces by the line, bricks by the song, my rap/trap game strong
Stay in a medicated zone, cause I don't got shit to worry about
Cause now my money long

Oversaturation I'm rising like inflation
I'm about to take over the nation
Total domination, it's a celebration over here
Yeah, Yeah it's a celebration

Control

My eyes stay feasting, should have optical diabetes
Beauty all around me, eye candy tests me daily
Do you really think you can defeat me?
My mother was an Evangelist, taught me the spiritual way
Serving God not supposed to make your pleasures less
Sin only occurs when you continuously do the same thing in excess
Like doing the same thing, thinking things are going to change
Can't shoot yourself and not expect to feel pain
Can't go outside during a storm and not get wet unless you have my last name
Mother Nature is my cousin, Father Time is a friend of mine
I frequently have to remind myself to return from amongst the stars
Jake Arietta of the game, no hitting y'all hall of famers
Got something more like a museum instead of a garage
Doing what i got to do to excel, trying to get rich like Seinfeld
Jay Leno cash, all wood but digital dash
About to burn another stack every time the lighter flash
Smoke when I'm bored, life is finally good, Praise the Lord
Playing both roles of the student and the teacher
Not policing these hoes, got a crowd of them like the Wrigley Field bleachers
Stay hitting home runs, saty catching pop flies
Not trying to live my life under the gun, gonna roll stay in control
And make this money like I just moved a ton
Complex like an algorithm, intellect of a mathematician
Music has always been my medicine, in high school I was a musician
Been writing for a long time perfecting the craft,
Soaked up the game, learned from my past
Stay smoking but never losing focus
Vision might get blurry, but that's when I crack the window so I can focus
Smoking on something that looks like the color of a purple Lotus
Got to keep my game tight, pack a punch like a stick of dynamite

Distracted/Life

What I should have been doing all this time, is writing these hits
But you know how it goes, got distracted by life's bullshit
Working all day, smoking all night
Ride the bus so much driver's know me on sight
But now I'm whippin, VIP sippin
Shooting pool in the Villa, smoking on that killa
What i should have been doing all this time is getting this money

But life is full of tricks and alot of them aint funny
Gotta go hard if you really want this money
Be on your P's and Q's, don't get played for a dummy
Counting checks, icy neck got mad respect
And oh yeah, I almost forgot , mad royalty checks, bitch!

Don't Want The World

I don't want the whole world, just give me an Island
So I can really do my thing, live my life in private
No fly zone, only one authorized is my pilot
Got a radar tower so no boats can come around it
Don't need no privacy fences, nobody but who I choose to be a witness
Fun in the sun all day, spend the whole night, smoking it away
Living life like a vacation, nobody but a select few know my location
You only arrive by invitation, and that goes out only to a select few
If you pretty, then I might next you
But until I get my money right, I'm gonna have to text you
I put on the Armor of God ao I can go to war
I want everybody saying I ain't never seen nobody go so hard before
Never know what's behind my closed door
Trying to do things that's never been done before
Smoke a blunt on the Moon, hanging on the Capsule door
Maybe make drink, on the Ocean floor
Never catch me wearing pink if it not for a charitable cause
My life is full of flaws, but i've gained from everything I've lost
I've paid the price, almost to its highest cost
Gonna take a whole lot for my heart to defrost
Don't want the world, I just want to be free
Don't need the whole world, there's enough for you and me

Finally

Finally found a way to express myself
Went a long time watching others accumulate wealth
Listened disinterested to a a lot of uninspired rhymes
Want that Lebron James money, not a jealous bone in my body
Want diamonds the color of honey,
Invite nothing but models to my private parties
Should have already been a rich man,
But life conspired to stop me

Could have been the dope man, but life had something different planned for me
Sold a few bags of crack, sold a few bags of weed
Wouldn't give a day back, these are the times that created the man you see
Did a lot of dirt in the streets, chased a lot of skirts in the streets
Well versed in the streets, cut like a brand new pair of cleats
Let's play a game of hide and seek, have you missing for a hundred weeks
Lost a lot of friends, made a lot of new memories
Making a lot of ends, I guess that means a lot of new enemies
Knowing when to save and when to spend
I manage my money intensively
Finally found a way in
Took matters into my own hands like Jordan in the Finals

Fortress of Solitude

Stay lit like a furnace, drink way more than I should
Just because I don't have a playlist
Don't mean I don't got respect in the hood
They tried to raise me as a lamb
But I got kidnapped by them wolves
Know how to defend my land
Go to war if the reason is good
Really don't want to do no interviews
Don't want everything I do to be breaking news
Wanna go out and get drunk, smoke a blunt if I choose
Rock some ice, live the high life
Swim in the deep end of the pool
Don't make me act a fool
Trying to keep my cool
Use my enemies as my footstool
Got power like a pneumatic tool
Drinking on a Green Apple Twist
Never heard of it before?
Because i just invented it
Green apple soda, cinnamon fireball whiskey
Been smoking on some good
Feeling so misunderstood
A warm pair of arms would really feel good
Help to take away the stress, I carry a lot of it on my chest
Helps to remember that I'm blessed
I don't know what's going to happen next
But I know that everyday is a different test
Trying to get a higher mark, trying to be the very best

On my castle walls, is where eagles nest
Fortress of Solitude, get higher than cruising altitude
Get quite rude if you play with my food
Trying to stop me from eating is like trying to stop me from breathing
Beat you like a heathen, colder than the polar season
In one ear and out the other
Save that shit for your other lover
Just wanna smash sometimes, no strings on each other
Play with that ass, hit it fast
No need to get under no covers
She stay wettin up the sheets, I stay wettin up the streets
Killing shit like the police, but I just want to find some peace
Find a way to release my grief
Been through way too much, fuckin around in these streets
Set you on fire like funeral pyre
Make you quit the game and retire
Nothing short of perfection is to what I aspire

Fuck With Me

Do you think you can love a nigga like me?
Come to the crib, make you my wifey
Trying to leave it alone, smashing different chicks nightly
Got chicks mad, some of them want to fight me
Smashing dykes, taking they wifey
Never met a nigga that got the game like me
Dive deeper than a whale
Fly higher and faster than a private jet
Always on that paper trail
I'm trying to show y'all now I'm as good as it gets
Build a house just for my pets
Build a house just for my guests
Got a nice estate, I stay grilling steaks
Boat out back by the private lake
Can Am Spyder rider, slingshot look like a jet fighter
Maserati on auto pilot
Smoked too much now I'm stuck
But my guys got me and all of our guns are silent
Stay toasting to the finer things, don't want a Testarossa
Give me everything with them wings
I got a hood mentality, spoil you like a cavity
Make you feel special, give you everything you want

God chose me to bless you, let you hit the mall and stunt
Let you push the whip, let you pilot the mothership
Stay freshly dipped, hotter than a geothermal vent
Highly successful experiment
I know that you were heaven sent
Don’t want to play no emotional games
Back and forth like tennis
But I do hope you stay thick, looking like Serena Williams
I’ll leave the game alone quick, and we can settle down like the pilgrims
Played enough games, loved and lost
Not saying no names, my whole past isn't full of pain
Had plenty of good days, had fun
Was company to a few with a pretty face
Sipped Moet, drank Grey Goose like it was water
Pass the blunt, get one back
Drinking straight out the bottle
Petty cash just to stunt, burning money just like the blunt
Drink so much beer, I might just buy a brewery then sell it for the profit
I don’t think about feeling fear, I keep a missile in my pocket
Hope the 2 of them thinking about doing me
I got a big stick in my cockpit
Bring her close whisper in her ear, don’t tell her what she want to hear
Tell her the truth, lean back and let her think about it
In a few moments, in a blink she gonna be all about it
More than words I’m trying to show you the truth
Want you to feel me, I won't hurt you
Love everything about you, we can stay fly like lovebirds
Show you the real me
When it hurts is when I prove I love you
Giving you nothing but the very best of me

Girls, Girls, Girls

Pretty girls, girls, girls I wanna love em all but I can't, huh
Pretty girls, girls, girls I wanna love em all, oh yeah
Pretty girls from all over the world I wanna love em all, Ooh
Pretty girls from all over the world, listen to this song

When I see you out shopping at the mall, pretty girl
Wanna pay your tab, show you how I ball, pretty girl
I just wanna show you love, so later on I can make that call, pretty girl
I’ll pick you up and we’ll go out to eat
In just one night Imma sweep you you feet, pretty girl

I'll have you saying you never met a man like me
By the end of the night Imma have you on your knees, pretty girl

Pretty girls, girls, girls, I wanna love em all, but I can't, huh
Pretty girls, girls, girls I wanna love em all, oh yeah
Pretty girls from all over the world I wanna love em all, Ooh
Pretty girls from all over the world listen to this song

When I see you in the club, smelling so good, pretty girl
Gonna spit that game like a real playa would, pretty girl
Buy a couple of drinks, have you feeling good, pretty girl
Slip to the whip fire up a blunt of that good, pretty girl
Now we in a zone, just the 2 of us, pretty girl
You touching me cause you can't get enough, pretty girl
It's almost time for us to leave this place, pretty girl
Grab your girl and lets head back to my place pretty girls

French Girls get freaky, Spanish Girls get manish
Australian Girls in bikinis, Black Queens in spandex
Japanese Girls in leather, Irish Girls in the Pub
Phillipino girls, the South Seas pearls, man I just wanna love
All the Pretty girls, girls, girls i wanna love em all, but I can't, huh
Pretty girls, girls, girls I wanna love em all
Pretty girls from all over the world I wanna love em all
Pretty girls from all over the World listen to this song

Good Morning

Good morning to all my haters
Better hope I don't catch you later
Got bitches catching the vapors
Hit you with the regulator

I feel like I got a lead shield surrounding my heart
Can't too much of nothing make me feel
Pimp oil in my veins, got the game from the start
Ain't nothing better than keeping it real
Wax on, wax off Miyagi drills
No tax when that champagne spills
Want that Kush and a couple molly pills
Tried to give you everything

My last name with a wedding ring
Now my heart is colder than the season before spring
Time to say goodbye, about to spread my wings
About to have a lot of flings
Sitting down eating dinner with Kings and Queens
Smoking blunts with the realest,
Lethal weapons I conceal it
Trying to follow the Spirit
But the world is so loud, that I can barely hear it
The weed is so loud, that my car, I can barely steer it
We all up in this crowd talking, but I can barely hear it
No man or animal walking, I don’t need to fear it
Got acres of land that i be walkin,
That’s why i be disappearing
Trying to make more than a living
Like everyday christmas or thanksgiving
Smoke a pound of kush like it was midget
Baby girl, if you got a bush, then i don’t want the digits
But if you got a pretty mouth, then I just might go ahead and kiss it

Good morning to all my haters
Better hope I don't see you later
Got bitches catching the vapors
Hit you with that regulator

A lot of people gonna say I ain’t never seen him touch a gun
A lot of people gonna say, I ain’t never seen him smoke a blunt
A lot of people gonna say a lot of different things
But I really dont give fuck, y’all can miss me like a strike 3 swing
Put your whole body in a sling, put you in the middle of the ring
Beat you till you bleed, please dont fuck with me
Never know who I got with me
Keep some blow and a glock with me
Won't catch me drinking Hennessy
It’s either Grey Goose or champagne, bout to do the damn thang
Ain’t a damn thing changed
Except the addy and the zeroes by my name in the bank
Let y’all stay caught up in the fame
I bet yall I got the game, dishing out pleasure and pain
For my baby everyday, Imma make it rain
Ready like the Clash Of The Titans
Ready like Ragnar Lothbrok on Vikings
Beat you like a young Mike Tyson
Trample you like herd of Bison

Travel the world like a nomad
Sail the 7 seas like Sinbad
Never find another with a larger set of gonads
Make you disappear like slimfast
Was far too lazy for first period gym class
Sleep till the afternoon, keep a Beauty Queen in my room
Get higher than a weather balloon
Mysterious like a distant moon, all eyes on me when I walk in a room
Changed the game, cause I got tired of playing the same thing
Now it's private planes, my girl got Gucci pearl strings
Lois bags, Chanel tags, smoking on good gas
Not worried about some of my past
Imma make sure you cum first, while I'm smacking that ass

Good morning to all my haters
Better hope I don't see you later
Got bitches catching the vapors
Hit you with the regulator

Grown Man

I'm on my Grown Man shit, not worried about a silly bitch
Quick to grab my shit and dip, sorry I had to flip the script
What your feeling is a seismic shift
About to drop yall into the abyss
You can throw any pitch, I bet I get a hit
They gonna call me a myth, stay smoking on a fat spliff
If she fine then I'm on her quick
Stay cleaner than a brand new stitch
Got game like Ben Simmons, coming thru with bad intentions
Hop out the whip, banana clip extensions
Far from weak, I'm the strongest thing you see
Give you enough rope to hang yourself
You should have used it to better position yourself
Now all of this wealth I'm giving someone else
You were focused on yourself, put our love on the shelf
I took the cue from you, started looking for something new
Love is a game for 2, too bad it ended up times 2
Had to add another next to me, just like you
Handle any situation like a Grown Man

I Was Just Thinking

She is my everything, She is the air I breathe
Without her, there is no me
We exist inextricably

Everytime I see your face, my heart does something I can't explain
In your eyes I see my face, and in mine you see what you can't replace
Keep me safe, take care of my heart, till death do us part
When I watch you move I love the way you glide across a room
Your poise and physique are so beautiful and unique
I long for the day that i can hear you say
I'm what you've been looking for, my heart can truly be yours
Don't say no more Mi Amore
I love you, and I hope you love me too
Say that you do, fairytales do come true
And it will always be me and you

I'm Limitless

I'm limitless, I'm limitless
I stay on my grind, man fuck a bitch
I been trying to tell her to get in
But i guess she wasn't feeling my shit
So now I'm limitless

Should have got in where you fit in
Now I'm beating new pussy up like Mike Tyson
Backyard parties, with every vice and sin
Please forgive me when it's my time for judgement
Play the cards I was dealt, no Russian Roulette
Might see me fly by in a Corvette
Or in a Mustang that ain't came out yet
Keep a bitch wet like water faucets
Had my dick kissed, said I was the best she ever met
Walking on every set, ain't a place that I ain't been yet
When it comes to the CHI, I look you dead in the eye
Tell you the ins and outs, Real Niggas know what the CHI about

Stay on your toes, only trust a few souls
Keep a blunt burning like coals
Please tell me y'all still burning Dro in Optimos
What y'all know about The Castle, or 62nd and Lowe?
62nd and Wood, shout out to Englewood
Marquette and Ellis, hustled up on Perry Ellis
Greenwood, in the middle of the hood
Back in the day don't look nothing like today
Used to live on Phillips,had family in the building only reason they didn't kill me
Only G on the premises, shot up the crib tho, made us move out yo
Made me realize my potential tho
One man alone is 1000 strong, 500 in each palm
I swing like I'm KIng Kong, smoke till it's all gone
I don't see nothing wrong with getting a little paper
They getting high off my vapors, another CHI Town Player

Justice

What does it mean,Justice?
The ruling of the Supreme Being, Justice
The right that overcomes the wrong,
Hear it ringing out in every word of this poem, uhh, Justice

The battle cry of the people, No Justice No Peace!
At war with the beast, to all the fallen Youth, may you rest in peace
We all know the police get a pass in the streets
Shoot an unarmed youth, go to court then get released
Paid vacation or administrative leave
Tell me , when will we see the freedom that was promised?
Still feels like slavery, The Police are the plantation owners
Speaking out with bravery, might just cause controversy
Did I go there and mention slavery?
Sure did, they killing with impunity, they got diplomatic immunity
Adding misery to our communities, they sell they lies fluently

What does it mean, Justice?
The ruling of the Supreme Being, Justice
The right that overcomes the wrong, Justice
Hear it ringing out in every word of this poem, uhh, Justice

Seeking Justice for myself, taking it upon myself
Cause i won't ever get no help

Staring back at a killer, standing tall as a Roman pillar
I'm gonna stand and deliver, best believe I'm nowhere near a quitter
Searching for equality, I'm trying to hit the lottery
But I can't let it bother me, smash the stereotypes like pottery

What does it mean, Justice?
The ruling of the Supreme Being, Justice
The right that overcomes the wrong, Justice
Hear it ringing out in every word of this poem, uhh, Justice

Looking back at all the things that have happened in the past
The tragedies of families that have lost by the fire, and the flash
In my eyes, i see the prize
Exactly why they point at the sky
Even then if you see me cry
Probably because I got blunt smoke in my eye
I've finally found the best way to find my own Justice

Keep It Real

On the beach under the umbrella
Sippin lean getting some Pussy
Smoking on that cookie
I'm hotter than a Mink Sweater
I got the game I'm far from a rookie
Hitting one bitch from the back
While she eating another bitch pussy
Taking over the game, call me a bully
Spilling champagne while I'm movin my money with a pulley
Been known to rock alone
Been known to not come home
Stay gone like a loan
May not answer my phone
Stay cleaner than a new gun
Get all my drugs together by 1
Spend the day getting on one
Spend the night fucking on one
A lot of you niggas obviously a lot richer than me
But I don't give a fuck
Cause I got game like I'm the son of Milton Bradley
Get it cooking like Steph
Made the game harder like James Harden

Isaiah Thomas in the fourth quarter
The Game is my Boston Garden
Write with rage like Russel Westbrook plays
Like the Lopez twins make you take a second look
Rising like a Phoenix Sun
Disappearing like a Wizard
About to grab the cash and run
Claw you like a Raptor
Now your King is captured
Hit you with the Clippers
Casket with a picture
Rip to all my enemies, when you die it might just be because of Me
Causing panic in the industry
Wait till they get a load of me
Causing pleasure and pain like pure cocaine
I'm sick like sickle cell
I'm on my way to Heaven i just busted out of hell
Not afraid to speak my mind
Letting itt shine in every line
Letting it shine in every rhyme
I bend space and time
Last of my tribe, I contemplate daily pulling a homicide
Catch a body or two then slide out
I know exactly where to hide out
Make you swallow a bullet along with you pride
Sexy ladies always down to ride
You know I'm reppin CHI
No other city meaner, and I say it with pride
Catch me slidin thru on Lake Shore Drive
Or on Stony Island getting high
Please don't make me get violent
You in trouble if I'm silent
Cause my emotions are on autopilot
Chasing a skirt to fill the hurt
Women don't know a real Mans worth
But that's another story
Claim the Game as my territory
Throw you off the 4th story
Fuck all you haters, y'all bore me
Money thick like a Redwood
Got a super plug, I stay smoking good
Mami thick, and she looking good
Balling like a pickup game in the hood
Old school whips, pockets full of chips

Just might catch me flexin, hangin out in Texas
Or hanging out in FLA, sippin lean smoking the night away
Pussy is my kryptonite, hit it slow after a dirty sprite
Pop a pill, smoke a joint
Keep it real straight to the point
Knocking the world off its axis
I'm coming up like tax brackets
Lil mama fine but she plastic
But I would fuck her up something drastic
Drinking out of platinum cups
Nigga fuck yo plastic
Being broke is not an option

Keep Me

Keep me in love with you
Make me want it every single day
No jealousy or secrecy
I want to be involved in your life, in every single possible way

We can make love at night
When it's raining, or the middle of the day
We can fly away like a loose kite on a windy day
Popping bottles of vintage champagne
Strait to the yacht, from the private plane
Vacations in Venice
I want you to feel me like a solo violinist
Stay praying for forgiveness
A lot of mistakes I've made kept me from handling my business
Feel like I got a repealed sentence
A chance to know what true love is
I don't want to know anything but this
The tender kiss of your perfect lips
Hearing you say "I Love You"
Nothing can compare to this
Willing to let you have your say
To keep my pretty baby happy
I'll do my best, whatever it takes
Quickly learn from my mistakes
Don't want nothing stopping us like brakes
Haunted by your lovely face

There could never be another that could ever take your place

Keep me in love with you
Make me want it every single day
No jealousy or secrecy
I want to be involved in your life, in every single possible way

You can run with the girls
Cause I wanna run with the guys
But we know how to do
When it's time for just us 2 to ride
I don't want the world for me
I want to take it so I can give it to you
If I can't give it to you to rule
We can travel it, everywhere we go
Act like it's spring break in Cancun
I got a mean vertical, but I don't need it to jump the broom
Trying not to get misty eyed
At the thought of you being your groom
My heart is a mansion, and I want you to use every room
I got a healthy love appetite
And your about to be consumed
It's all about the pleasure I get
From seeing your pretty smile
I try hard to hide the butterflies
I get whenever your around
Take my time speak slowly
I want you to really know me
Don't want to sound lame or phony
But I want you for my one and only
Build a bridge between our hearts
Link them for eternity
Till the end of this life
I promise to give you all of me

Keep me in love with you
Make me want it every single day
No jealousy or secrecy
I want to be involved in your life in every single possible way

Late nights or early mornings
Trying to find the best words
To tell you how I really feel about you
Don't let no one tell you different

This is really all about you
You've changed my perspective of how love should be given
You are my vision of perfection
Take my hand please say you're willing
Trying to change your life
Show you a better way of living
Trying to change your last name
Give you all of these millions
We all know that sometimes love can be a cold mistress
But I got the secret to the game
Keep it locked up, deep inside my brain
Sorry y'all, but I can't share everythang
But I will share my heart with You
Let's heal each other from all past hurt and pain
Give you my hand to hold
When we walking down the street
Want you to lean on my shoulder
Any time that you feel weak
Never seen a beauty so rare
In my eyes you are truly unique
A living breathing work of art, a Masterpiece
I can't believe that you belong to me
Cleopatra reincarnated, beauty can never be overrated
Especially if its outwardly radiated
That's when Pretty and Beauty get seperated
Don't want you to be gone too long
I love it when your by my side
You roll them dam blunts better than me, girl
Come on baby, lets ride out and get high

Keep me in love with you
Make me want it every single day
No jealousy, or secrecy
I want to be involved in you life, in every single possible way

Let The Games Begin

Didn't think that I would ever gra a pen again
Thought the game was over
Thought I had lost my chance to win
But as long as I have breath
I'm betting on myself
Gotta welcome the sunshine in
Open up the curtains

Pull up all the shades
I got what can ease your hurting
Like a Sunday morning organ
I'll make you say, "Oh, God"
Leave you satisfied for certain
Let the games begin
Wanna fuck just because we can

(phone rings)
Me: Hello?
Her: Hey, what's good?"
Me: Shit, I'm in the middle of something right now
What's good with you, tho?
Her: Nothing, I just wanted to come over
Me: Now's not a good time, I'll call you back later
Her: OK
Me; OK
CLICK
Let The Games Begin

Lie Steal Cheat

I'd lie, steal, cheat just to be with you, girl
And I know you feel the same way too, girl
I'd lie, steal, cheat just to be with you, girl
And I know you feel the same way too, girl

Let me take you, to my private room, girl
So we can do, what we want to do, girl
Leave your troubles right here at this door, girl
And I'mma take you, right here on this floor, girl

I'd lie, steal cheat just to be with you, girl
And I know you feel the same way too, girl
I'd lie, steal, cheat just to be with you, girl
And I know you feel the same way too, girl

Let me take you all over the World
We'll make love on all the foreingn shores
I'll show you things you've never seen before
We'll make love like never before

I'd lie, steal, cheat just to be with you, girl
And I know you feel the same way, too, girl
I'd lie, steal, cheat just to be with you, girl
And I know you feel the same way too, girl
I'd lie, steal, cheat just to be with you, girl
And I know you feel the same way, too, girl

Let me buy you diamonds and pearls
Just say it and its yours, girl
I'd lie, steal, cheat just to be with you
And i know you feel the same way too
Let me fulfill all your fantasies
I can be everything you need
Just put all of your trust in me
And we'll make History

Living Hard; Who Knows About This!

Have you ever went to look for food
And found nothing but maggots instead?
Have you ever got ready to go to bed
But the hotel you was living in caught fire
Then you had to evacuate instead?
Have you ever been homeless
Nowhere to call your own
Didn't fall victim to the loneliness
So now the whole world I roam
Have you ever had to share 1 toilet
With 100 other niggas?
Have you ever been locked up
Dreaming about them figures?
Heart locked up, I'm a NWA typa nigga
Yeah I'm using that word
Cause when you yell, you always get heard
Have you ever been to a month of Revival?
Summer camp, learning the Bible
Learned at an early age
Never let my hands or my mind be idle
Don't worship no idols
Don't kill unless it's vital to my survival
Vitamin Packed, pain resistant
Don't like to cut no slack
Give an inch, they wanna take a mile

That salt pinch, then I smile
Crocodile that just caught a hippo
Pockets fat, stay flicking a Zippo
Went from nothing, to a whole lot of zeroes
My list is short, I don't got too many heroes
Stay living hard
Whether I'm walking, on the bus
Or whippin in a foreign car
Not trying to be a superstar
But you can't hide from your ability
Love those who are kin to me
All the rest are my sworn enemies
My words sting like a swarm of killer bees
Lyrical death in this poetry
Loyalty thick like a Redwood tree
All of my riders stay high and fly like me

Living hard, life don't give no favors
Take it in all it's flavors
Stay sharper than a barbers razors

You would think we was playing laser tag
The way I got the scope on you
Got a lot of people mad
But that's on You
Imma make it do what it do
Options like 1a, b2
No stopping cause I'm on 1
You should be 2
Lived a rockstar life way before it was cool
Some days in my real life now
I be broke like a rusty tool
But I work hard and my mind is sharp
My living is hard
But I'm in the hands of God
So the sands of man can't make me fall
Slow me down, all my enemies fall
Secret haters and well wishers
Bebaters and false information pushers
Looking for a come up
There was never a run up
Or you would have got done up
Bad situations kept us apart like segregation

An obvious situation, let's have a successful operation on the patient
Cause for celebration, time to Boss Up
Got a few coupes, but beware when you see that black truck
Cause we strapped and bout to blaze up
Not talking bout no weed
Y'all niggas better take heed
If you ever feel the need, do what you gotta do
But I'm quicker than you, plus I got shooters in my crew
Stay in your lane, let the King reign
Like biting down on a bad tooth
I'mma cause you a lot of pain
Didn't have to go in the booth to spit the truth
Got em numb like caine
Yeah I got a lot of nerve, when I drink and drive I don't swerve
Like dirty sex, but i'm no perve
When I'm in the mood I splurge

Living hard, life don't give no favors
Take it in all its flavors
Stay sharper than a barbers razors

Doubt it if you want, leave you stuffed in a trunk
My heart don't know no fear
My mentals got me killing shit like Metal Gear
Call me Man Of The Year
Show up to the club in a Lear
I'm cold hearted now, so I've frozen every tear
Thought we could build a dream
But nothing is ever as good as it seems
Bank account bursting at the seams
Stay rottweiler mean, that's the Gemini in me
I eye everything skeptically, make moves pessimistically
Improved my situation exponentially
Y'all might have to grab a dictionary
I'm something of a visionary
Make my girl sing like a Canary
I'm an OG like Jason Terry
On the path to greatness, got an excuse for my lateness
Had to experience life so I wouldn't come with no fakeness
I know what it's like to be the object of affection
And I also know what it's like to feel the fire of rejection
But no matter what I'm going thru
Like when its snowing, I stay cold like an igloo
The Florida sun couldn't melt my heart

Now my pain got me on top of the charts
Living a hard life got me prepared for dark nights
No water, and no lights
Going to jail with no bail, solitary nights
They say they want to pick a fight
But they can see it in my eyes
They ain't about my life
Savage and civilized, street runner but baptized
Spiritual power, physical strength
Mental ability, not an opponent you want to go against
You'll get jumped like a fence
Make you wish you nerve started shit
I'm not a snake, so I don't hiss
Death is as silent as a Lovers kiss

Living hard, life don't give no favors
Take it in all of its flavors
Stay sharper than a barbers razors

Lyrical Rat Race

Don't side eye me, don't lie to me
Don't feed me poison in my IV
Cause your beating heart is connected to me
I feel every pang of treachery and jealousy
Empathetic, telekinetic, highly energetic
My destiny has finally manifested
Dog off the leash, bitch I came to wreck shit
Spent too much on my necklace
Smoke too much gas, I'm out here reckless
Imma get a passing grade every time you try to test this
Please don't be mad if your name not on the guest list
God has Blessed it, the Game I direct it
My name they respect it, don't end up on my check list
Or Imma leave you neckless
Wreck you like a foreign car, then go cop another
Go back to the same bar
They wishing on Me when they wishing on a star
Smoke weed by the tree, keep my weed in mason jars
I'm a friend indeed, my real friends know who they are

Walk past you like you ain't there
We don't breathe the same air
Go to the trunk and pull it out like a spare
But the trunk is in the front, and it got a whole lot of thump
It would be too easy, to mention Donald Trump
So Imma keep talkin about that lemon squeeze pump
Cash stashed away like water in a camel's hump
A nigga came to play, so baby girl fix your lace front
Make sure your looking good
Cause I wanna knock on it like wood
Love them girls from the hood, that stay smoking on that good
Don't get me wrong, I done smoked reggie before too
Fuck lyin on my smoking and fucking habits
Aint always been models on my mattress
But now I charge like a high rise in Manhattan
Or a Chitown condo
Real G from the streets, let's get ready to rumble!
Stay on my grind mode, stay on my shine mode
Ain't got no time for a slime hoe
Put a bad bitch in the figure 4
Pop a tag every day
Got chips like I work at Frito Lay
Got plenty bitches want to lay where I lay
They might get the digits
But they don't know where I stay
My real house is somewhere far away
Put it in my wheelhouse, and Imma hit it far away
I been stressed out my nigga, now its time to play
Bring the toys out, save the drama for another day
Smoking on a pound of hay
Pop a molly fuck the night away
Sip some lean now I'm in another place
When I find my Queen we gonna move to outer space
Lyrical rat race, no way to say whos in first place, until now
I stay on that paper chase, Im good because i got amazing grace
The valley is full of shadows, the sparks from my pen
Burn bright like tallow
Been in the deep end I don't do shallow, been sick with the pen
I'm practically infallible
Smash a hoe let her know straight through the door, it ain't about the dough
But I'm rising like yeast, Yo
I'm on a fantastic voyage, the cause of alot of employment
The cause of alot of enjoyment
Don't make me be the cause of your funeral services

Put it where it needs to be
Tell the truth don't lie to me
Not about the industry, just trying to find some real G's
Who wanna fuck with me
The whole world is my pen
Bout to be where I've never been
Just like my smoke blow my cares to the wind
I don't care what it costs because I got a lot to spend
Been on party mode since I don't know how old
System on overload too much liquor too much smoke
Too many to chooses from to poke
Like em thick as fuck classy but fuck ratchet
Although on any given night anything can happen
All that ass clappin, and I just happen to see it
On some real life G shit, Imma put it real deep bitch
Make it jump like a hydraulic switch
Imma hit it out like the first pitch
Love the way she walk, she got a mean switch
I love a pretty chick keep em on my wish list
Rat race pull of in a cloud of smoke
Life ain't funny, real shit aint no joke
She want a lot from me so I made sure Im never broke
Open hole for me to poke ass pussy or throat
Sorry but it was murder that I wrote
Keep em numb like coke
It was only truth that i ever spoke
Say my name like a chant, my money grow old school like a Chia plant
Or should I Say pet, I'm a rookie and a vet
Keep a tech on deck, but I don't mind slitting your neck
Im Orkin and yall the pests Im killing yall whole nest
Not worried about what comes next cause there ain't no such thing as second best
RAT RACE

MAMA

For all the departed Mothers, Especially mine She Was So Beautiful

Mama
I know you raised me better
Im sorry Im living this way
But since you've been gone
I've felt so much sorrow
And I've been living out of these bottles

Mama, oh Mama How I love you and I miss you
Mama, oh Mama How I love and I miss you

Empty cans everywhere
And I barely care
How I look or what I do
Cause I'm in a daze, feeling half crazed
Cause I'm always missing you

Mama, oh Mama How I love you and I miss you
Mama, oh Mama How I love and miss you

I drink til I'm sober, drink till the night is over
Drink to forget, another Queen like you I never met
I pray for you love from heaven above
I remember how you struggled
To make sure we had our needs
But I was so selfish
Never thought about paying the rent
All I thought about was me
All I ever did was stick my hand out
Never tried to give anything back
Now that you're gone I'm stuck writing this poem
I remember Easter Sunrise Service
Early Easter Sunday morn
Even now that I'm grown and Im on my own
I still don't understand why you have to be gone

Mama, oh Mama How I love you and I miss you
Mama, oh Mama how we all love you and we miss you
To my sisters and my brother, to the rest of my family
This is for all of us I LOVE YALL

Man I should Be

Man I should be gone by now
But a nigga still here
I use that term as only We can Black MAn to Black Man
Don't want to see me with a strap in my hand
Don't want to be on T.V.
Travel the world, smoke like a Rastapharian
There he go in a foreign again, either whip or country
I'm the bully, so you could never punk me
I see through you like a cloud
Smoke way better than what you got now
Not trying to draw attention, so I got the silencer now
Walk the red carpet don't say a word just nod and smile
Top predator like we in the wild
Hungry nigga with a shark toothed smile
Bite you in half,I wasn't even hungry
Your futility makes me laugh
They paying me like GOFUNDME
Chitown nigga, wher I learned my craft, dont make me laugh
Been known to kick a niggas ass
Way back in the day, what yall call a trap today
Crack house livin, no shelter given
Cut you like a ribbon, no joke no Robin williams
Split it down the middle, a pie, cash or pillow
Don't lie kick that ass, solve you like a riddle
Man I should be on by now
But instead of typing I kept on writing
Get a rush, it's so exciting
Elevating my life and doing the most
Exercise her body like a ghost
Paddle in your lake, eat you like some French Toast
I bet I bench press the most
Money in a backpack, my pockets cant fit all that
I spit like hot wax, fuck with chicks with fat cats
Redbones delicious, chocolate makes my wood fat
In the crowd inconspicuous
Smoking chocolate and she got one to match
If you think you can run with me, then show me your my match
If not then Imma be out like a gust of wind on a match
Man I should be doing better, but I'm trying my best, no vest
Run in silent circles, know niggas that will murk you

Not to mention what I would do to you
Push right through, fly like a witches broom

(ME) Been Drinkin Again, Oh Shit

I said I wouldn't drink no more
But every time I hit the corner store
The cheap bottles of beer, whisper in my ear
And tell me let's explore the depths of my mind
I can't find when Im sober
Then I find myself wanting more and more
Far from being sober, I'm on a rollercoaster
Can't leave this shit alone, mad when all my drink is gone
Sippin too fast, can't make a case last
Drinking like a V12, grab another bottle from the shelf
My wife gets mad, takes the keys to my Jag
Cause she don't want me to crash,
Another bottle in a brown paper bag
Drinking hard on my days off trying to forget about my boss
And no choke my co workers
Man I hate it when I have to be sober
Trying to ease my pain, a little alcohol always changes the game
Makes me feel like I'm immune to my pain
See the world through a glass half stained
Go walkin in the rain for a 5th of any thang
When I crack the seal, no more stress and that's for real

Moment of Silence

Can we get a moment of silence for the rap game
Because I just killed it
Took a lyrical AK and emptied out a full clip
No more getting away with bullshit
Now yall niggas go to come with some heat and some substance in yall lyrics

No more getting away with barely spitting make a hook most of a song
Most of the time a beat is the only thing that saves a song
Stop me if I'm wrong, but I don't plan on stopping
Here to get this shit poppin
And I will never conform, I'm a man half gun
Old school like Voltron, aint another nigga better walking under the sun
Meaner than a rattlesnake, beat you till they cant recognize your face
Going all in, in this paperchase
Trying to leave a legacy that can never be erased
Trying to build more than a Dynasty, trying to build a Monopoly
Manage my money properly, watching all the niggas who be watching me
Watch my stock steadily go up, keep a full ass cup
Always ready to kiss lady luck
She gonna end up sprung if she let Me fuck
Beat her like a cop with my nightstick, love it when she's on top
Watch her make faces while she rides the dick while i play with her tits
Got the whole world i the palm of my hand and I just might not share it
But that's not how I was raised, a thug with manners
Hanging up Da Vinci portraits in my home like championship banners
Blow up your head like Scanners, nail you with the hammer
Shoot you like a camera, feed you monkey ass the whole fuckin banana
I go green without the gamma, holding myself to a higher standard
Like a responsible parent I make sure I get all my lettuce broccoli and carrots
Most of yall niggas is parrots repeating eachothers rhymes
Some sneaky like ferrets never wrote a line in they life
Not gonna apologize because I'm good at writing rhymes
Not gonna apologize because your girl wants to read between my lines
Im crippling niggas taking they heart soul and spine
I'm good with both the triggers and figures, this is the end of yall line
This rap game is mine, a lyrical mastermind only 1 of my kind
Like Jor EL or Optimus Prime
If I put on all my ice I might make you go blind
Got you reading this again like you just pressed rewind
Harder than a diamond tip, I just loaded up another clip
Chillin on yachts that look like cruise ships, Maserati the color of cool whip

Pay somebody to make my clothes, don't want to wear what y'all wearing
Yall niggas dressing like hoes, rock my own shit, save my fucking dough
I'm richer than a corporation owner, turn you into an organ donor
Split you like the lime they gonna put in my Corona
Never been to California got to make my way out West
Shout out to them city streets, when I come hope that we don't make too big of a mess
I plan on partying with the best of them, forget about the rest of them
Pretty women, always trying to get next to them
Fuck niggas you know we got to flex on them
Shining like a flood light in the middle of a dark night, keep my swag air tight
Don't need no bitch fuckin up my night, dont need no bitch fuckin up my life
I'm looking for a lady that I can love and treat her right
The kind that rolls over and wants to get hit in the middle of the night
The kind I would have took home to Mama so she could meet my future wife
In these lyrical olympicsI just got the 1st, 2nd and 3rd place finish
The whole world is a witness on how I just handled my business
So can we get a moment of silence for the rap game
Because I just killed it, took a lyrical AK and emptied out a full clip

One Man War

It's gonna be a one man war if I have to ride about mine
I'm not calling nobody up Imma roll out solo
Strapped up like Columbine

No innocent lives taken, aiming with precision, target taken down
Legend born like I’m Jason
A 1 man wrecking ball, blow your brains out against a fuckin wall
Leave none of my enemies alive to speak my name
Bringing a shower of fire and pain
Got several clips on each hip and a couple in my belt and they all legal
Straight evil, Wild Wild West shit, not a nigga you wanna mess with
If you good then we probably mesh quick
But if you snake then you gonna get your head chopped off, bitch

It’s gonna be a one man war if I have to ride about mine
I'm not calling nobody up, Imma ride out solo
Strapped up like Columbine

To the critics that see these lyrics and attempt to label me
Psychoanalyze my rhymes, try to find out the who and why
This aint for nobody in particular, this is for ANY fuck nigga
That think against me they gonna be winning
Money is the mission, y'all can keep the world
Respect to the streets real niggas and pretty girls all over the world
From the burrough to the suburb, from the city to the country
The mountain top cabins, and the secret homes tucked in the valleys
Got plenty of places to go, plenty of shit to see
That's the only thing thing that can interrupt me
While I'm finally living my life carefree
Took my time forgot how to rhyme got back in the lab now I got a fat ass slab
I'm from before the age of the dab, I’ve seen a lot of shit
And I've seen a lot of come and go fads but grab the cash while you can
Sink some Yen in the japanese stock market
Do a few numbers so I don't have to go back to the bank for at least 4 summers
Living life everyday like its the middle of the summer
I’m heavy like the total weight of an all chromed out Hummer
Business man that was born in the hood
Make money, don't see it, act like its not even there
Got cash in more than just 1 stash, closet look like Jumper
But I got hammers and thumpers and sprayers and thunder
Got plenty of ammunition to take you whole team under

Don't get me started with the knife play
Walk past slit your shit and keep walking with a straight face
Im tightly laced not a stitch out of place
Shoot that pussy in the face, in the streets and the sheets
And you'll probably never see me again

Pocahontas

Saw her standing by the jukebox
Searching for her favorite song
She had on high heels and a Mini
Man I never seen a pair of legs so long

She looks just like Pocahontas
I think I seen her in my dream
She looks just like Pocahontas
She looks so damn good to me

Saw her out there on the dance floor
Dancing to her favorite songs
Man I wonder if shes tired
Because she been dancing all night long

She looked just like Pocahontas
I think I seen her in my dream
She looked just like Pocahontas
She looks so damn good to me

See her standing by the bar now
Taking shots of alcohol
And their doubling up her orders
Because its time for Last Call

She looked just like Pocahontas
I think I seen her in my dream
She looked just like Pocahontas
She looked so damn good to me

See her walking towards the door now
Humming to her favorite song
Then she tapped me on the shoulder
And said I know you want to take me home

She looked just like Pocahontas
I think I seen her in my dream
She looked just like Pocahontas
She looked so damn good to me

Now its 35 years later
And we got grown kids of our own
And everytime we go dancing
She plays her favorite song
She still looks just like Pocahontas
Stepped right out of my dream
She still looks just like Pocahontas
She still looks so damn good to me

(Promise) More Love

Gimme some more
I need some more
I gotta have all your love
Hey Baby
Gimme some more
I want some more
I gotta have all your love

Give me your heart, and I'll give you mine
And I promise everything will be alright
Hey Baby
You do your part and I'll do mine
And I promise everything will be alright

Gimme some more
I need some more
I gotta have all your love
Hey Baby
Gimme some more
I need some more
I gotta have all your love

Gimme your time
And I'll give you mine
And I promise everything will be alright
I finally found what I couldn't find
Now everything's gonna be alright

Gimme some more
I need some more
I gotta have all your love
Hey Baby
Gimme some more
I gotta have some more
More of your love

Quick

Don't want you to think that I only shoot on the court
Or when I'm in the booth, Got Deadeye aim
Shoot you from across the street on the roof
Or walk up to your face let the Bushmaster loose
I just proved you wasn't bulletproof
Always looking for that 100 proof
Always looking for my roof
Pull up topless but its a 4 door not a coupe
Ladies want to play with me
Everybody want to know the scoop
Where he from in the CHI, how the hell did he get this nice?
Got the game cooking like a pot of white rice, got a lot of ice
But that's really not that important
Stay overseas, get a lot of shit imported
Living like a real Don, Playa status
Don't forget where I'm from
Chicago Pimping, if she not the one then my heart gone
Stay missing, if she not the one then we not going to be kissin
But if she the one then Imma make her my mistress
Causing explosions like a pyrotechnician
Causing careers to end and begin
Bout to give the game what Its been missin
Im literally a beast in the kitchen,
Lyrics that you got to read again
My niggas make you pay attention and listen
Probably thinking its unfair how fast I took over
Got majic like a Wizard, bury you like a blizzard
A whole lot of cash, and my green look like 4 leaf clovers
Over in the Swiss Alps riding around in Rovers,
Allen Iverson crossover
Hall of fame got to make room
Humbly asking Tupac and Shakespeare to scoot over
Another all time great just got allowed to enter the room
Hitting so hard and fast messed around and caused a sonic boom
Street fighter like Guile,promise to drive you wild
Don't take much to make me smile, beat you like a bad child
We keep the heat just like a dryer
I think I might just stick to the weed, I'm not trying to get much higher
But I will sip something that got me moving like a snail
But even that can't stop me from continuously chasing this mail
Got Kush in a garbage pail

Sto;e her heart like a thief now my ship can finally set sail

Dumb It Down

My mama told me to dumb it down so yall can understand me
Not doing this shit for awards ya'll can keep y'all Grammys
All I want is the money
Got the game on lock, only a locksmith can understand me
Pressure cooker, smash they ass like hookers
Yeah I'm a looker, but I only got eyes on one
Baby girl let's have some fun stay lit just like the sun
If you aint never been, fuck it we about to be on one
Stay smoking strong Stay getting that money
Stay overseas with my honey
She don't want nothing but time from me
Yeah I work the hardest stay smelling the best
Stay on your mind make you forget about the rest
Like a pick up game I got next
Stop yall like a teflon vest, make you my logo like Jerry West
Don't want it if its too hairy, like it smooth as your breast
Suck it like a bottle have you cummin like "Next'!
Leave your ex vexed like an angry bird
Have you singing all night that's my word
Do it hard but I won't make it hurt
Trying to live under your skirt
Eat it like dessert, let me give you what your worth
No dollar amount exists on earth

Me Going In

Put the pen to the paper as the same time i put the flame to the joint
Sippin on Bacardi dark wishing for love in the dark
Another journey on the ride called life, Lets go
I'm about to embark for some reason I gotta keep it moving
Need that one that can run with me
Don't want to cuff me to no chimney
Cause I stay high, so I'm always looking down
Thats why you see me smile when I should have a frown
Hope all my haters drown, but then again I would let them live
So they could carry their mistakes
Then I would be inclined to forgive but never forget
Mind as fast as a Corvette, push myself to the limit
Of a normal man got enough energy to do anything I say I can
Swag like none other, bat 1000. Louisville slugger
They all want me to be their lover
Of Course I got enough to call all they bluff
Leave em stuffed they cant get enough
Stay on my huff and puff trying to blow a pound down
Run with a crew that don't need to make a muthafukin sound
Smoking on something way above what you people call loud
Sorry to say it but yall sheeple following the crowd
Do my own thing I am the Lord Of The Rings
Championships,poppin bottles and clips
Trophy Wife winners life, my secrecy can cause an eclipse
Never know where I'm at Could be having dinner in a spaceship
Yall niggas got paper with no imagination
Lazy minded money blinded my blindfolds off
What I want is mine, yes
Don't give a damn what it costs
Not worried about what they think, I go my own way
I know my shit stinks that's why I spark it so they can smell it
Don't worry about tomorrow, tonight I'm trying not to regret it
Put it where it needs to be, between what I consider family
Mind blurred, speech slurred, mind of a nerd
Not afraid to admit I'm smart, missed crossing the stage because of a credit in art
But the rose that blooms behind my eyes keeps me more than alive
It helps me to thrive, I strive to create a better place
Than what I found, when I leave I don't know if there's joy or not a sound
Grown man, boy been lost and found
Looking for a girl thats ready to be a woman now

Stay on a search for peace, knowledge and a better me
Mates come and go, unfortunately thats just how life goes
Love gets you in its highs and lows
Make you regret that you proposed, makes you love her forever
Turns your heart into an umbrella,Loves storm can produce crazy weather
I love the days of freedom, but they just don't understand how i choose to move
Im at the center of a crowded room made of my people and my goons
Eating off of titanium spoons, my cranium got maximum room
IQ higher than a witches broom, Good night, Drop the Mic

Question

Is this a flickering flame? Or a raging inferno?
This is the question that burns eternal
Do you love me or do you hate me?

We used to ride like Bonnie and CLyde
Just the two of us, out doing us,smoke a joint till its dust
Drink a couple of beers then slide off in the cut
Used to beat that pussy up, known to get in them guts
Even if it was only once, got caught reminiscing
Trying not to gaze too far into the past
Let it go like a lost bet because i'm the best you've seen yet
Killing shit like a Green Beret chopping money like paper mache
Slingshot Maserati, turn it into a 4 seater
Collect dimes for a hobby nigga buds green like Wasabi
Keep a heater stay hidden like a lost treasure
Vacation life I go where ever
Catch me all over the place might pay to go to outer space
Got a crib under a lake separate the real from the fake
Keep it real make no mistakes
Niggas show they hand and they cant see that You see they snake

Question
Is this a flickering flame or a raging inferno?
This is the question that burns eternal
Do you love me or do you hate me?

Never jump without a parachute
Money around my waist like a fuckin hula hoop
Stay playing with the loud, smoking making my own cloud
Solo like an only child, never pay attention to a petulant child
Fly by in a wingsuit money taller than the chimney on your mansion roof
Everything I want I do, but I keep it classy
That's exactly the differences between me and you
Get pushed back like the sunroof spittin 1005 proof
The gas made me do it got me lit like molten fluid
Beat that ass like Lennox Lewis
Mind fast as a speeding bullet, know your move before you pull it

Question
Is this a flickering flame, or a raging inferno?
This is the question that burns eternal
Do you love me or do you hate me?

Am I bearing my soul for nothing? spilling my life in this ink?
Paradigm shift paradoxical gift, I call it a curse
Cause everytime I spit I can't miss
Golden like the light of the sun, done with negativity
It's time to have some fun
Put you in your place look you dead in you face
Leave you dead in your place, Kep plenty cash in the safe
Got the game on red alert Like a ThunderCats Tshirt
They gonna have to go back and rehearse
While I keep hosting rhymes in reverse
Create a singularity in the rap universe
Put a bunch of shit in my bitches purse
Smoking on some shit, blue like a smurf
Cash like a GM, bitches be like yeah, i know him
Swim in my ocean, drown you with my emotion
Take a sip of my potion, I bet I get your devotion
But Question?
Is it real or ist the financial appeal?
Do you cumm off the dick for real?
When I lick it do you really get a thrill/
Is it because I'm rich?
You really need to answer this Question

Is this a flickering flame or a raging inferno
This is the question that burns eternal
Do you love me, Or do you hate me?

Distant

Tell me how we became so distant when we both right here?
Can't help but shed tears heart full of hurt and misery
Trying to move forward sto reliving history
Take the good with the bad, but life comes at you in waves of multiplicity
Telekinetically controlling the game, killing em even more
Because I'm not in it for the fame
Keep a blunt burning like a Cali wildfire flame
Do the damn thang, won't leave feeling no shame
Cant say its me to blame I'm just putting a flame to the game
Causing blistering pain scorching my name into the Wall
And The Hall of Fame
Shame on a vic that thinks that they can best this
Leave you buried, distant from your home
Pieces everywhere you die undiscovered and forever alone
Ponder your word carefully, don't provoke me unnecessarily
Do you something terribly, leave a mark indelibly
Competition like MJ, best not even try it
Cause a 1 man riot
Blow your eardrums out, leave you stuck in a world of quiet
Assassin mode, I'm always quiet
Move like a shadow but I'm far from shallow
As you can clearly see there is a distance between everyone else and me
Free style with no beat No stoppin, read it again for repeat
Gifted something vicious, throw you out like leftover dishes
Drain money from the bank spendin it on my Missus
Kush like grape now and laters
I bought a whole lot so I can smoke some now and later
Got a brand new everything, watch, crib, whip
Stop, don't think it's sweet
Always got the game figured out, show you what it's all about
Play for keeps, all I take I keep
It's the dual yin and yang, the push and pull
The blast before and after the bang
Got a crib that's not a crib at all its actually a bank

Rabbits

I saw this one girl and I was like Oh, My GOD!

I wanna hit that all the time like Rabbits
Take you back to my city, give a good girl bad habits
Imma buy us a patch of land and with you I'll share my cabbage
Anything you want or need you can have it
As long as we doing it all the time like Rabbits

As long as we sexin all the time like rabbits
Baby your body all the time I gotta have it
When I see you cant help but want to grab it
Stab it, lick it like an ice cream cone
Make you moan then make you scream,
Nobody can hear us so baby girl do your thing
I promise to make you feel like you never felt before
Like warm butter is how your body will melt for sure
I can't help but cum cause your soaking wet
Love playing below her bellt
It's a forest fire and I don't want to put it out yet
Say my name again, I love how it sounds, I love the way you say it
Like when the bed squeaking when I'm ponding you down
No neighbors for a mile so we getting wild all outside
Nobody know where we at
And I'm hitting and we kissing and I'm sticking
And we both body licking, going all in and it's just the first round
Beat it like people feet when they stomping the ground
Now you sleep, hope you ready for another round
Imma wake you up in a little while
So we can do it again like rabbits

I wanna hit that all the time like rabbits
Take you back to my city give a good girl bad habits
Imma buy us a patch of land and with you I'll share my cabbage
Anything you want or need you can have it
As long as we doin it all the time like rabbits

Let me play with it like a PS4, and I'll be your remote control
We smoking and we drinking so we bound to lose control

What i be thinking when your not around
Is how I wanna lay your body down, kiss you from head to toe
New sensuous spots found that you didn't know you had before
Generous with our lovin, we keep it on fire like brick oven
Thick but not fake Single lady? What a waste
I will chase but I'm a wolf so I got patience
Catch you when you get tired of running Then imma keep you body cumming
Dip my dunkin stick in your milk get it super soft and wet
Make you feel like your dreaming I know I got your body steaming
Ready to let me in, but I'm not ready yet
I want you to keep going, like a rabbit,all night imma be at it,
As long as you say I can have it
At time Imma be gentle and at time Imma beat it like a savage
Like we in a tribe, in the forest, order a thousand roses from the florist
Spread them on the floor, Rose Petal Love
All over the living room, sexing from night till noon
We didn't even make it to the bedroom
Cause we on sexcation, your body is my celebration
Your the nurse I'm the patient, with you I go crazy
But I'm rich now so I can afford to be lazy
Kush got a nigga feeling crazy stay feeling on her booty
Give it to me again baby
I wanna hit that all the time like rabbits
Take you back to my city give a good girl bad habits
Anything you want or need you can have it
As long as we doin it all the time like rabbits

She let me push it like a foriegn, our sex is never boring
She didn't even know that she was snoring
I take a shower then I'm back in the game like Jordan
Now she up taking her shower, I'm flaming up the sour
Take a shot getting ready for round 3, I love baby girl company
Cause she let me hit it constantly and she as beautiful as can be
I done fucked around and got so damn lucky
Scored the game winning shot, now I got my trophy
Love pulling on your hair but I know not to hurt you
Keep you up all night because neither of us has a curfew
You will be one of the select few to witness how I handle my business
Keep you missing like a trial witness, now she wants to be my Missus
Hitting it like big league pitching, positions we'll be switching
When I kiss her there, she say that it be tickling
Playing with a beautiful body is my hobby
Hate that I always have to pick them when they in the lobby
But I'm moving around like the tide, but we can get back up later tonight

And imma beat it up again like a championship fight
Then I gotta catch a flight, but if you good enough you just might jump on the mother ship
Now you got mile high status
We all up in the clouds, she getting super loud

Rampage

Stay getting higher than the trade winds, Bae prettier than any Mercedes Benz
Stay razor sharp never no loose ends, go straight to the stash if I want some loose ends
Damn I'm back at it again, backyard session
Me the drank some weed and my pen about to upload another lethal injection
Pure power makes up my essence, my punch like a shot from a Smith and Wesson
Do whatever it takes to keep surviving, know when to fly high and when to go diving
Nothing short of my reality, past present and future history
Can't blame the game on me, I just got way more than others
Like I got a key to every city, RIP to Whitney Hate I never got the chance to meet you
All the legends that are gone you'll live on through my poems
More than just the beats they sang on, the words they sang meant everything
They knew how to speak of love made you want to go out and buy a ring
Made you shed tears that you didn't mean to
Reach back over the years when the words hit your ears
And suddenly your back in time Walking around touring old memories
Rewinding time in your mind, the influences to paint a vivid picture
Live in the music, Keep going like a truck with no brakes
Smashing through the bank wall trying to loot it
I'm the best kept secret since Draymond Green, MVP of my team
Shots will have you sleepy like you been sippin lean
Hotter than a heatwave keep a hottie off in my mancave
My D tighter than Gary Payton back in his Glove Days
Stay searching for exotic strains to take away my aches and pains
Physical and emotional, got way more than enough love for the both of us
Even if you put me out in the rain my love for you won't ever rust
Just because of my demeanor people mistakenly think that Im greener
Than a granny smith apple, but I can be sour like a 10 year old snapple
To get the best of me, we gonna have to grapple

I'm way more than what you see, I know a lot of people who would cap you
Stay chasing them dollar signs, stay chasing them ladies that's fine
So much trouble has been mine it's about damn time
Shine like freshly polished silver, no its not white gold or silver
Leave a bad taste in your mouth like liver,
They find your body bloated, floating in a small river
Just like the mailman I deliver, on point like a fully stocked arrow quiver
Got a hair pin trigger, death blows are what I'm prepared to deliver
Cause more pain than alcohol in the eye, or severing your main vein
If this thing is do or die I'll be the last man standing
Like a gladiator in the arena, blood soaked but crowned as king
Take a good look at what it means to have control of everything
If I see it then its mine, don't want to argue or waste no time
Bowling ball smooth yall niggas gutterballs, utter fools
Pay homage to those who earned it
Teach the game to those who need to learn it
Roll the blunt right so that it don't burn quick got gas like I got stock at BIC
Quick to smoke a fat stick puff puff pass like I know magic
Way beyond the norm I'm like an electromagnetic storm
My magnetism attracts mostly wrong, but I'm barely right myself
Can't judge no one else, do a lot of things by myself
That's why I can keep my feelings on the shelf, to myself
Always looking for weed greener than Seattle and meaner than the 12th
Turn an RV to a party bus and tour the country by myself
Love the freedom but hate the lonelies,but im running it like Tebow, stay away from the phonies
Only the realest can phone me, trying to build a business like Sony
Futuristic like a photon stun gun, dismiss the myths I really been on one
Waiting pays off in the long run, crushing shit like Fat Joe and Big Pun
Ladies loving me like they favorite re-run
Showing ya'll how the game is supposed to be won
I'm not surprised Im supposed to be number One
Humility and extreme belief in Me gave me the strength to take on the industry
Goy a lot of length, got some history behind me
If I looked into your eyes you would probably be afraid of me
Being a Gemini is a great source of pride
It allows me to see both sides of things at the same time
Two hearts being ruled by just one mind
Differences in tastes, but both all about that cake, do whatever it takes
Im immune to the poison of you snakes, love to burn like well done steaks
Want a little honey, that's sweeter than frosted flakes
Make me go through withdrawals, when your not around I get the shakes
Forever trying to recreate that night I got my first taste
Don't let a good heart go to waste, not when love is staring you right in the face
No matter whos right or wrong got to weather any storm

Better get freak like porn if that's what turns your lover on
Don't want to be watching it by yourself
We all know what that means, no need to say anything
Vintage like top shelf print my own wealth
No matter the heat I wont melt, save defeat for someone else
Make waves like the ocean, stay sippin on some kind of potion
Need one that deserves my devotion, blow her mind like an explosion
Takes way more than you know to stay colder than the Chi Town snow
To boldly go where few rarely get to go
Get to know people only a few ever get to know
Highly opinionated alienated highly debated and hated
Mad another brotha made it, didn't fold continued to play it
Blood cold, but a heart of Gold Staying in the game even if i need a tourniquet
Gaining crazy fame like I just won the NCAA tournament
Putting ya'll to shame make you wear the number 2 ornament
I can see it coming from a mile away G, somebody gonna try to intentionally foul me
Calling no time outs tho, clock winding down, pressure packed situation
Step up with no hesitation,waiting for the standing ovation
Line for the Championship Trophy Presentation
Don't want yall to feel like I'm being antagonistic, I'm just being a realist
I dont give a damn what you think I'm not real with this
A pen is mightier than a sword but my gun will send you straight to the Lord
Trying to find a balance, strike a perfect chord, I got range like a harmonica
Stay up late like I got insomnia
Got a lot of friends with ends, whippin in a Benz here we go again
Told me to let you go but you acting like we more than friends
See through you like an optic lens, got over you like a colonic cleanse
Touring like I got my own sports club, flying higher than a dove
Need someone different to lift my spirits
Like a jack, a girl that got my back, roll the whole sack
Know how to fix shit when it git out of whack
Play the game with no shame just as good as Goldie The Mack
Carrying the game like the Olympic flame
Positively helping put Chicago on the map again
True I been gone from home, but it will forever be where I'm from
Easy to rally an army to get you stung,but by myself I'm 1000 strong
Don't get it twisted because my hair is long
Want nothing by my side but Vickie Secret Model types in thongs
Smash like I'm naming a ship, need me a contortionist
Fold her body like my paper got the bed wet like water vapor
Pool in the backyard, a criminal with positive subliminals
Please keep the hating to a minimal, so we can keep the casualties to a minimal
Collateral damage caused by the jealousy
But the losses definitely not coming from me

Hit you like an avalanche, choke you out where you stand
Make no mistake about it I'm a grown ass man
Doubt it find out about it put you deep beneath the land
Game got her trapped like quicksand
Every since I tapped been begging for me to be her man
Like Biz, you say he's just a friend, I'm not sharing unless you got a twin
I guess I'm a male nympho, love it at any tempo
Fast as a Buggati or slow like a vintage Pinto
Let me go harvesting in your garden
But you gotta be cleaner than a brand new carpet
Caught between the streets and the sheets
I wanna fuck all th etime but I need money to eat
Scrooge Mcduck's lucky dime, smoke a whole pound of lime
Wisely using my time, brand new money shine
I'm not here to be seen Im here to fulfill a promise
Told my mom I had a dream got to go hard by any means
Wish she was here, thank you Jamie Fox,that song really helped me a lot
Determined to try to help, got enough to take care of myself
Time to help somebody else, so they can pay it forward
Make more money than a corporate lawyer
Smoking blunts as long as a lightsaber, drinking on a sour apple now and later
Kind of nerdy like a skater but love to rock some Gator
Smoke like a volcanic crater, trying to make outlandish paper
Drive you crazy like K2 don't think that nothing can save you
I'm on a rampage like a rhino, snap your ribs like old vinyl
Weed got me dancing on the ceiling like Lionel
Drowning yall niggas I'm tidal, see me going up in an upwards spiral
Killing it like I'm suicidal
Work ethics match the best in athletics
I got the insulin shots, the game done got diabetic
Laying on the table dying but I'm not about to let it
What you smell is me smoking the gas only premiumNo more unleaded
Part of me got patience part of me got a temper
Part of me love relations Part of me cold like Alaska's old Decembers
Give me what I need and I'll give you the best of Me
Vacation home in Tahiti got to fly over to see me
Face like KIm K, body like Lisa Ray, demeanor meaner than Serena
Hola, Bonita Mamacita, bout to find a co star for my mini feature
Occasionally i cross the streams, light and dark mix
Bacardi light and Dark, blackberry juice, shit strong as a bitch
Far from being crazy, I just like to drink
Smoke so much the room is hazy
Like when I sink deep into that pink
Been known to be a drinker, heavy smoker rarely catch me sober

Known as a deep thinker, roll over you like a giant boulder
Keep an Angel on my shoulder, the fire inside of me smolders
Keeps my heart from growing colder
No time to be afraid it's all about getting paid
More energy than a hand grenade, don't want her if she needs to be saved
Got to match my swag, ride with me, hide the pistol in your bag
Love to smoke love to pearl, love to let me poke I say kissing on her pearl
Know enough about the streets now I'm reaching for the stars above
Spent most of my life on my feet, wanna chill at the crib
Play the game smoke some bud
Get helicopter high, eat like i'm starving and I'm about to die
Ride in a coupe, hide a bunch of loot, haters get the boot
Partying like I'm a young Snoop, got a lot of pretty women jumping through hoops
Thinking I'm gonna buy em a whole lot of shit
All I wanna do is slide em a whole bunch of dick
Take my time and get mine but I want you to cum quick
Nothing wrong with love making time, doing some old erotic shit
Put you in different positions like we rearranging the room
My one and only I don't mind kissing
But you gotta make me want to be your groom
Make me want to go missing, just us on vacation
These things that I been missing, dig your body out like an excavation
Doing my best not to fall into all temptation
I won't settle for less than real love and dedication
Hidden behind the suit of armor, I'm just like Iron Man
But you cant see my armor, its inside guardian my heart again
Until I find 1 worthy to possess what I have
Imma party all over the world G, lowkey not really giving a dam
Mentals faster than a hummingbird's wings
Got talent like I'm standing on one hand on a balancing beam
Speaking of gymnastics I hope that you can bend over backwards
Hit it like a hole in one and I'm playing at the Masters
Take the love making to a whole nother level
Your body is the Earth and my body is the shovel
Baby girl shines like a thousand diamond bezels
Every time I see you all I wanna do is sex you
Time to put on something see through, let me come over and bless you
Take you in my arms show you that I'm for real
Take my time, don't cause no harm but I do plan on making a kill
Legs around my shoulders back arched like a cat
Want it early in the morning like Foldgers, kissing from your neck
All the way down your back, make the foreplay last for days
Eat it like a dinner from the microwave
When it comes to the bed room there's no need to behave

Want and want to be a love slave
Please always keep the kitty, clean and freshly shaved
Rock hard like a street that's freshly paved
Want something good to eat and your bodies what I crave
Let me rub your body I got the magic touch
Tub full of hot water playing in the suds
Or standing in the shower, water got you extra wet
Cumming hard like a water jet, dripping like a water faucet
While I pull your hair I'll be kissing on your neck
The whole time I'm there I want to explore your body like a shipwreck
Professor and student, no time for acting prudent
Eat it like a well done steak, I can feel your legs start to shake
I love hearing that sound you make, when I break your will
And there's not much more you can take
I'm feeling you like a pill and i got something as long as a wooden steak
I want to dive deep into your mysteries, crate som brand new histories
Trying to do things differently, but your body keeps tempting me
Take it to the kitchen hands on the counter, beside the refrigerator
About to switch positions again get up on the table
I don't care if it breaks I didn't like it anyway
Wanna play with you like a game of pinball
Like it's the last shot and I'm about to win it all
Trying to make your walls fall, but keep that thing tight and I'll keep coming back for more
Addicted to the love making, she is too she aint never faking
Want to lay you down like some tile, get you wetter than the NIle
Swim in your ocean for a while, leave you sleeping like a peaceful child
Nothing compares to you, nothing but stares when you come through
About to rip your dress in two, your sex got me always wanting to get next to you
Wanna take you home right now, let you leave tonight
When the sun goes down, been making love all day
Go home get you some clothes Take a good bath and change
See you in a couple hours, I'm about to do the same
And smoke a couple joints of sour, got me wanting some right now
Looking for you like a letter from a pen pal
No need to pretend now, we want each other badly Love you passionately and madly
The feeling I get when I kiss your lips, I can barely explain
Don't want it to be over quick take my time like a road trip
Got her body down pat like Mike with his eyes closed when he shot the freethrow
Barely anywhere I won't go, a one man audience getting a private show
Gifted like a god from Olympus, but had to take a different route
Trying my best not to offend any of them I'm just saying
I'm not playing a dirt nap is what you'll lay iEat you like a lyrical piranha
Strip you of all your pride and honor
Bionic man like Steve Austin, throwback to the classics

We on that Knight Rider shit

Rarefied Air

Never really been one to care what another motherfuker think
I'm breathing rarefied,keep my girl laced up in ice and mink
Rocking retro J’s made of gator take a good look at a real player, haters
Neck look like pack of frozen now and laters
Stay dipping overseas, I’m chasing global paper
Causing panic in the industry, not trying to make no enemies
I’m literally rewriting history pen full of blistering pain and heat
Hope dont nobody run up on me thinking shit is sweet
Know a couple of moves that will sweep you right off your feet
Combat ready fuck around and make me snipe you
Heavy like a 69 Chevy, hell yeah that's definitely a good year
If you a Grown Lady and you fine then i might pipe you
That's if I don't find The One first, then I just might have to wife you
Got patience like I’m all alone doing Tai Chi
I don't need a limitless pill, Mary Jane always does it for me
Super sharp focus although I can write totally sober
I'd rather be high, so I can share my rollercoaster ride
So much going on behind my eyes
I know i’m using more than 10%, more like 105
Got spiritual knowledge worldly wisdom, I’ve even been to College
My younger days I truly miss them
My life reminds me of the scripture
About the men being given talents two invested
One buried his and like him I almost lost my blessing
To whom much is given that much more is expected
Life buried my talent but i was allowed to retrieve it
Given a second chance about to take off nest believe it
Ladies all I ask is If I smash please keep it our secret
Got too much cash, peoples nosey ass
Build you up just to trip you up
Dont want to lose everything fuckin with some random slut
Keep my lady on my hip just like shes my extra clip
A lot of ice and chips fingers neck and ears, both wrists
Never will I forget my home I know those streets way too well
All over the city I used to roam either with a car full of people
Or riding through the city nights alone smoking on some good shit
Sipping on something potent had a hell of a life already
Compared to having fun money will always be secondary

But dont think that I'm not serious end up on a missing persons list
Walk past and drop a grenade in your casket bitch
It's how I will deal with potential enemies
You don't want to awaken the Gemini in me
The other side of me is relentless beast
Like a pitbull mixed with a Saint Bernard with no leash
Rip your whole body apart, make a mess scene
Leave the cops in shock cut your spleen out
Leave it in your mouth with a sock
Violent images thought process primitive
I just want to live in peace without fear of having to unleash the beast
A lot of people talk about what they capable of
I'm wise as a serpent but sometimes not so harmless as a dove
I done already drank a lot of liquor and smoked pounds of bud
I even made myself a cup of cherry and sprite mud
Drank that bitch at work and i was feeling good as fuck
Might fuck around and put 40 inches on a Jaguar truck
I'm out with my Beauty Queen and we both drinking out of golden cups

Small Promises

There's not enough ways to let you know how I feel
I've wasted a lot of days got to make up for it for real
So worried about other people's opinions
Time to worry about myself,this life is ours for the taking
Only us 2 when everyone else has left
Promise to love you to death, give you my last and final breath
Keep it spicy like a chef, never make you word about neglect
Save you from a broken heart never let us fall apart
Loved you when i first saw you had to wait till I could have you

Small promises to keep you always loving me
Do anything I can to keep you next to me

I wont find your happiness in a box at the store
We can find it at night at home behind closed doors
Or when we on our way out to eat
You singing me love songs in the car
Never want to be without you
I find myself thinking about you
Since the day I met you I could never forget you
Perfection personified your beauty got me mesmerized
Practically got me paralyzed every time I look into your eyes
I feel the butterflies start to rise
Thank You for bringing love back into my life again

Small promises to keep you always loving me
Do anything I can to keep you loving me

In a room full of precious jewels you shine like the brightest diamond
I would gladly be your fool do almost anything to keep you smiling
Trying to paint the perfect picture
Mona Lisa must have been your sister
My hearts been hit by a twister
When your gone too long i start to worry and miss you
Love it when i get to hold you tight and kiss you
This love making is officialTrying to tear it up like tissue
Don't want you to never have any issue

Small promises to keep you always loving me,Do anything I can to keep you next to me
Smiles

Smiles tell lies,got to look behind their eyes
The eyes can never lie, a lot of things hidden behind smiles

Watch out for the daps, watch out for the pats on the back
Watch a nigga eyes, see if they shift left right or back
Giving y'all game, leave a nigga brain as a stain
Watch who you smoke with all night
Watch who you kick it with, watch who you trust the digits with
Dont put your total trust in no nigga or no bitch
Niggas fake as paper mache, fake niggas need they life taken away
Lame niggas get their wives taken away
Gameless niggas got nothing to say
Spray like a sprinkler, make a mess call the Cleaners
I bet my weed greener, I stay fresh like I own a cleaners
God like demeanor, I see y'all as inferior
A rabid Rottweiler ain't meaner, I go Cujo with the meat cleavers
I'm a nightmare in the walking flesh, I'm already considered amongst the very best

Smiles tell lies, got to look behind their eyes
The eyes can never lie, a lot of things hidden behind smiles

You can buy all the weed, bring all the bottles
Make sure your crew got what it needs
But to some your deeds will still be hollow
Haters are like the stars, they always there no matter where you are
So I keep all 3 eyes open, see your spirit lurkin,
Im economy unto myself, pockets fat enough to go floating in the ocean
Haters can get the morgue shelf
Fresh like the new day, flesh like I was born in a forge
Niggas talk tough but are you really ready to meet the Lord?
Slit you with the Green Destiny Sword
Practice makes perfect, but acting aint worth it
Stay true to who you are, fuck yeah I would blast off
Knock you off put you in the family plot
Bulletproof I guess not, Smoke you like rocks
Pour your ashes on the block
RIP, you was never worthy, trying to battle me
Your gonna need your whole army

Stamp Of Approval

Hell couldn't take me, hell didn't make me
Hell couldn't break me, hell didn't make me

But this world did, bout to be rich as a bitch
Hit it like the last pitch, stand tall like Im 7"6'
Smoking big blunts burning my damn fingertips again
Stay trying to slip the dick to a pretty chick
Make it do what it do, stay on the hunt
Playing the game like MJ with the flu
I got Heavens stamp of approval
So I can stack my money tall as the tower of Babel
Up and down Jacob's ladder, where I go you cant follow
Fly like a Swallow, see me halfway around the world tomorrow
Got a team I lead, I ain't gotta tell them to follow
We in the place to be and we ain't leavin till tomorrow
People always underestimate me
That's why I can get searched by the cops
With an ounce of weed and walk away scot free
Didn't search me thoroughly
Didn't find the knives in my belt
Had plenty of weapons that I kept to myself
Know how to protect myself
Leave you in a position of regret
Don't want no sorry keep your respect
I keep my light shining and I know it's blinding
That's how I keep them demons in binding
Light bright, neck right, tech on site but let's have fun tonight
Have a blast do it big, smoke a pound reup again

Stop

There's way too many beautiful ladies, they all trying to drive me crazy
She looking like she would make a pretty baby, I need only 1 to save me
As much as I would love to love them all, my time is precious
And I don't got time for a million calls
Only 1 voice I want to hear,on the other end telling me she needs me near
My homey, lover friend
They see that I stay fly, they see that I stay high
They see that I got swag, they see that I got cash
They only want me for my money, Need one that's as sweet as honey
Don't want nothing but Time from me
Turn me into a better man, I've learned there's nothing I can't do
Cause when I found you, I knew that I could love again
And that wishes do come true
Work hard like a 9 to 5 to keep my baby satisfied
We all long for love, for something to feel something real
Something that fits like a glove but it's hard to find like steel
I'll buy the car let you take the wheel
Call you Misses Money Bags, now you got my last name for real
Baby I'll take the lock off the gate, let you sit in my private garden
I'm willing to wait as long as it takes
Because I know eventually all my love problems I will solve them
They see that I stay fly they see that I stay high
They see that I got swag they see that I got cash

Survive?

Could you survive, if you were forced to live on your own?
Would you survive, If you had to walk a country night alone?
Would fear over take you if you didn't know what your next meal would be?
Would you have the patience to put in hundreds of applications in a couple of weeks?
Have you had to sleep on the floor, because there was nowhere else to sleep?
A cover and a pillow on a cold cafeteria floor mice and roaches in the ceiling Mold on the walls?
Some of the things I've seen would have easily broken a weaker human being
But my spirit is strong, I pass my life energy along
Make everybody around me strong, Im positive like a solar energy storm
I got a lot of things to say, I got a lot of things to do
Please don't get in my way so I don't have to make an example out of you
A lot of people couldn't have survived my life
I've paid my dues and life paid me back with the gift to write
A lot of insight and a lot of empathy,
That's why sometimes I can seem like I don't have any sympathy
My pen is something like a symphony or a brush painting a picture, or crating a haunting melody
I keep my head up but sometimes I find myself feeling melancholy
Sometimes I need to be alone, let my thoughts run wild
Astral project I'm a Star Child

Thank You (In Advance)

Sunshine soaked streets weather pretty much always nice
Nothing can be sweeter than strolling them with my wife
Got to hold her hand to help her carry the ice
Not another better in the land, everything about her perfect in my eyes
Hair, body,, nails face and eyes trophy wife I got first prize
Angel that gave up her wings nothing but a blessing to my life
Just as strong as me, not afraid to jump in the whip and ride
Taught her how to shoot, know we stay on our Bonnie and Clyde
She loves to smoke, drink just like me
Pretty Lady thank you for loving me, in advance
Thank you for giving me a chance
Thank you for a life of romance
Someone to buy flowers for, someone to love care for and adore
She's cotton candy sweet, without you I'm incomplete
Like a lost and lonely sheep thank you for coming to rescue me
Thought that love was a myth, didn't know that it could ever feel quite like this
Like the pulse in my wrist my heart beats for you
Your honey sweet kiss, soft and silky lips
There's nothing I wouldn't do for you
Your my Lois Lane and I'm your Superman
Your my Mary Jane and I'm your Tarzan
Together for this lifetime, giving you all my love and my time
No one else is in my eyesight, your the only one in the world I see
Thank you baby, in advance
Swallow my pride put the pimp game to the side
When a Beauty and a Beast collide, undeniable chemistry
Never take you for granted, treat you like your the only woman on the planet
Sweet like a forbidden treat, stole my heart like a master thief
Love to greet your eyes every sunrise got a hold over my mind
Feeling like a helpless child
Love is so strong makes you run into the storm
But like a glove real love is always warm
With you I want to build a dream home, let you design it how you want
Put fountains in the front, plant you a garden full of different color roses
Baby your my hocus pocus, making your heart happy
Make you smile everyday treat you good emphatically
Please you in every way
Giving you the very best of me let the rest be history
I got cloud 9 on earth, she got 9 ounces in her purse
Let me show you what your worth, I will always put you first
Baby Thank You for loving me, In Advance

The Storms Inside

Picture standing in the desert, a sand storm on the horizon
Your the only survivor, the wind itself is violent
What would you do? You cant outrun it because the wind is way faster than you
Go back the way you came but everything looks the same
The sand burns like a flame makes you cry out in pain
And then you roll over, shaken by another dream
You wonder when it will all be over success isn't everything it seems
But right now I wouldn't know because i haven't tasted it yet
But I have had a pretty decent life ran the streets with real G's
Back in the day when everybody had fire ass weed, huff didn't exist
Everybody in the CHI had that piff
Smoking on something that smelled like cat piss
Those are some of the things I miss about home,
Chi Town, Stand Up Grow Up Man Up
Please Do You But let them do them too

Thoughts On A Friday

Walk up in the spot looking magnificent
All gold everything like a world class olympian
Then I got my platinum days when i wanna rock them blue and grey J's
Of Course I can afford Versace but I'm not cut out to be a carbon copy
My defects make me one of a kind, got a different frame of mind
Channel my inner chi so to outside bullshit I'm blind
So basically you can't really get to me
Say or do what you want just don't send too many threats
Cause 1 is too many stretching the boundaries of respect
Like an elephant I never forget
We all live and we learn a lot of us sit and we burn
Keep a cup of something cold nearby, watching the time fly
Try not to trip over my pride ready to run the streets and ride
Flawless women by my side, lawless is how I live my life
Smoke while I'm in a red state, they trying to call me a reprobate?
Oh, I guess I'm just imagining things, I know the thoughts of most basic human beings
Look at you one way, talk to you another
Smile dead in your face but behind your back cursing you Mother
Those the type of people I want to smother
But Imma keep my hands to myself till its time to put somebody on the morgue shelf
Really not trying to go there, just letting yall know I'm far from scared
Should have been dead, got more lives than 9 cats
Smoke a pound to the head, tighter than an official snapback
Wrap her around my finger in each others presence we love to linger
Should I put a ring on her finger?
She already got ice on all her other fingers
That 1 is conspicuously missing like exclusive love making and kissing
We walk around pretending, instead of fences mending
Looking for greener pastures moved on from all the old laughter
New face to look at new feelings to feel
Hoping that this time the love is for real
But on the flipside where them killers ride they far from colorblind
Everything you do is magnified, what you saying
Knowing how to act dignified, knowing how to make money multiply
Know all about the fallen angels in disguise, Promising heaven but got hell in their eyes
Like the morning sun I rise, wet like the morning dew she greets me with her thighs
Please don't act so surprised, y'all do it too everyday and every night
Grind like a wood chipper, shine bright like the Big Dipper
What I feel like at the moment sipper, heavy hand held pistol gripper
Just because I love Women y'all niggas betta not take it for a weakness

It's a race for the money like the Preakness hit you like a tackle dummy
Never show no signs of meekness ,You can catch me out doing me
Maybe ChiTown New York or Miami, Cali love Texas mud
Smoke some bud in a Tennessee valley
Should have never lied to you, although everything I said wasn't untrue
Should have done better by you, now it's too late cause the past i can't undo
Stuck sitting here with a bunch of memories, nothing but a bunch of broken feelings
Didn't think that it would really get to, now half the time all I'm doing is existing
Lost my reason to love, now I'm out here dolo
Struck like a lightning bolt from above, back playing the game lIke Marco Polo
Searching and looking like Im in the kitchen cookin
Looking for that perfect spice so my dish will come out extra nice
Don't want nothing less than the best, why settle for less
I'm heavy in the game like a 800lb bench press
Got a
Lot of style but I pay less, came a long way from shopping at payless
Its the reason why i don't smile and I say even less
Broken heart don't talk they lay silent outlined in chalk
Truly my spirit is willing but pain makes my flesh weak
I know I'm not done giving but I need to receive equally
That's hardly ever the case, Keep something burning close to my face
Need a cutie sweeter than red velvet cake, strawberry cheesecake ice cream good
Sophisticated lady that was born in the hood
Kill For you like Charles Bronson, stay fly for you like a young Don Johnson
Ride in the sky with you, get high like The Green Monster
Got to take my time go out and perfect my grind
Make sure nobodyLights burning brighter than mine
Baby your body belongs right here next to mine
Got that desire to move around, have fun under the sun
Get wild like Gronkowski, smoking blunts on a Jet Ski
If this is what you want, your gonna have to catch me

Truth Being Told

Sometimes I think I'm beyond repair, caught in the grip of misery and despair
Feeling raw and open like a nerve
Ceiling falls and hope withdraws, nobody here to help me this burden bear
Vulnerable moment, truth being told
Wasted a lot of precious moments, let go of a lot of hands I promised to hold
Always searching for that special someone, I probably had her a long time ago
Looking for the horizon,out in the ocean on my boat
Can't seem to find what I need to ease my mind
A friend that loves to ride out, love to go out but love to hide out
Loves to smoke out like burnt bacon, shake that ass like a Jamaican
Wine for me baby give me some love and save me
Please dont treat me so shady, trying to drive me crazy
Won't settle for nothing less than a lady, maybe we can raise a baby
I've settled for less but GOD saved me, I've bettered myself
Now look what GOD gave Me
Trying to make sure that you have everything you need, give you everything
But it does come with one string, if I feel your capable of handling everything
My heart in a box in the shape of a diamond ring, want the shine in your eyes to be only for me
Love it when we ride and get high, through the fog of life your the only thing I need to see
Me and you together would be like breathing underwater
The impossible just happened, cherish love and adore ya

Try
I Know yall gonna feel me on this One

I try hard, to be a Man amongst men,
Work harder than the next nigga push mysel get it in
Stand out without talking, people want to go with me me when I'm walking
If you good with me, then we not walking
And if I feel like you dont like me then you can keep walking
Always catch myself watching the square box talking
Random bits of reality get in Tragedies from overseas
And at home affecting how we living again
What's the point of bombing innocent people?
Say whats on your fuckin mind and maybe somebody can help you
But after cowardly acts only GOD can help you
We coming to get you and I bet that's the one thing we're not gonna have to try to do
Talking about the Red White And Blue
The colors that link you to me and me to you
America the Beautiful or America the desolate
Obama made history and I feel like he gave me the opportunity to spark about unity
Man even though he out of office we have to try to keep
His message of hope change and peace going perpetually
I never saw the need for greed, o the reasons for being selfish
You have to be to a certain degree, but not when you become extremely wealthy
Imma dress just as cleanly but on a more regular basis
Thats about it for the changes except for the diamonds
And a return to only drinking champagne
Celebrate life in the best way you can,We have to learn to respect life again
Like newborns, have to learn how to treat each other again
Not saying you have to bow down to another man
But we are all masters of our own space, boundaries that can never be replaced
Once crossed that's where we make the mistake, situations escalate
And sometimes murders take place
Maybe its the weed got me thinking about a better place
Somewhere I can enjoy my day without a care no trouble in my way
I try to keep my karma clean so when it's my time to shine
Imma be flyer than an Eagle's wings

Unfair

It's incredibly unfair, that something so lovely and uniquely rare
Can't belong to me I often stop but try not to stare
I see You often, but I don't even care
Because everytime I see you it's like a breath of fresh air
I don't ever press the issue, when your not around I miss you
Never got the chance to kiss you, cherish every moment that I spend with you
Something i would love to hold something I would love to watch grow old
Someone I would forsake all of the world for, someone to go to war for, or with
Someone that would appreciate my heart as a gift
See so many, that fit that description, but nothing but 1 drives me
That's one of my life's missions, to finally settle down find a wife
Stay at the crib throwing down in the kitchen, smoking on extensions
Loving the life that I'm living, no point in having it if your not willing to be giving
Your love and your time, baby girl your light shines brighter than mine
No distance or time can ever make you leave my mind
It's unfair that i can't call your name got me out searching in the rain
Stay looking in a beauties eyes so she knows I'm not telling her no lies
No need to do that, baby girl back yard like a cadillac
Shopping sprees with fat stacks, where you at baby, where you at?
It's unfair That I can't find true love, been in Love a couple of times
But that thing is strange, it truly is blind, looking but not really
I know yall feel me, just a glimpse into the real me
Hoping as always that one day GOD forgives me
I stay patiently waiting doing what I gotta do
Cleansing my heart from hating, nobody in the world has the same view as You
Waiting for my Guardian Angel to save me
Until then i gotta face the world alone, bravely
Strong just like Atlas, I haven't got tired yet, got the strength of a jit but the savvy of a vet
I'm as unique as anyone you may have ever met
Mind got scalpel sharp focus
I'm trying to be the best thing going and I want everyone to know it
Got chicks circling like satellites in my outer orbit
Hoping that I might choose, hoping that I might wife her and buy her anything she choose
Don't want to come off rude but I'm far from a young fool
I'd rather walk alone than be used like a tool
It's unfair that the beautiful girls are always taken,talk just for the sake of conversation
Love to hear your opinions and views,
We got a lot in common you love a lot of the same things I do
Too bad that somebody has already claimed you
Just goes to show that there's more than one type of Angel
A true friend in need, is a true friend indeed

On top of that baby girl your gorgeous, curiously I'm not jealous
I go on about my business, never giving a clue
Maybe a hint here and there but what's a man to do?
It's so unfair your so unique and incredibly rare
Love everything about you, your eyes body and hair
If you were mine we would create our own sunshine
A love like ours would be one of a kind
But as always I keep searching for what I may never find
Until then smoke and get this money
One day Imma find a real Woman who wanna take a lil something from me
Not just for a moment, if I feel your the one then your gonna know it
If I don't, tell you I'll call you but I don't
Moving around like the Jet Stream, stay high as the Jet Stream
No such thing as impossibility, but for now Imma let you be
Love how you move your body to your own unique beat
When I look at youI see a vision of ecstasy
Dude must be a fool, because your standing awfully close next to me
I could see myself loving you passionately
It's unfair that you can't belong to me

Want You

When you want to go in but you can't, people thinking you don't go hard in the paint
Angel wings dirty from the world, smudges on my face from kissing too many girls
Trying to find new things to give you, other than diamonds and pearls
I could try giving you my heart and giving up all them other girls
I see it as a start to you becoming my world
Nothing is more precious to a man than his girl
Fire and desire, trying to take us both higher
Fly you in my arms like SuperMan, you gave me the faith to believe I can
Give you anything that love brings, a house a dog kids and a ring
Stay focused on only you, stay faithful and true to you
Waiting for the day That I can say I Do
Love knows no time or place , has no tasteHas a power that can never be erased
No better feeling other than GOD's Grace
She is so amazing that no one could ever take her place
And if for some strange reason my words don't reach you heart
Then it wasn't our season
Now I'm all over the globe, leaving a trail of smoke
Hitting a lot of hotties, when it should have been all about her
Sliding like mud, might catch me with a cup of mud
Most likely Im drinking something I can chug
Star spangled blunt, I got the red, white and blue
Wishing on a star to get my heart wherever you are
Told you what was on my mind, silence for a reply
Dont know what to think make a nigga go and drink
Smoke as much loud as I can get my mind off the bullshit
Stressing like I'm on trial and they not about to acquit
Coming with that legit shit, pimp shit i know yall feel it
Game on point like a fat ass zip
Garcia Vega smoking, green game blowing Ice House sippin
I'm in the zone I'm trippin, trigger finger spittin
Competition dismissing I stay on a mission
Crash my spaceship order another one from Mars
I don't go to boujie bars, catch me in the hood shooting pool at the local bars
Walk all over, then see me driving in the same day
Never know which way I'm coming put buckshots in your face

Warning

It's just me and little mama doing our thing riding out
We smoking hella marijuana, got them diamonds out
Shining like a lighthouse, from ChiTown to NY
On the West Coast, Imma stay fly
I might not smoke the most but i promise you i stay high
Got cash on demand, don't want you watching me like cable
Got a chill spot in Japan, drinking Sake at the kitchen table
I can take care of myself better than anyone else
Seems like a simple statement, until you think about the dependants that
Take away from our self maintenanceYou no longer have time for yourself
lSeems like success has a bitter taste to it
I'm hunting megafauna lyrically, trying to be the best to ever do it in history
Seismic shift in the game, I rule Empirically
Got a Beauty Queen and she completes the Royal Family
Recreating ancient dynasties, about to sail around the 7 seas
About to turn it up to seven hundred eleven degrees
Make the game uncomfortable make you quit and want to leave
I keep a cannon up my sleeve, want paper like I'm half man half tree
It's the before and after, both sides of me
About to add another leaf to my family tree
Stole the game like a thief, now it's all about me
I'm MJ in Lebron's body, nothing you can do to stop Me
96 Bulls good, all the rest is copies
Travel the world but you can't take the ChiTown hood out of me
Got a chip on my shoulder, I feel like I been looked over
Let the flame in my pen game smolder, cooking up a fresh pot like folgers
Don't want to have to come face to face with a real soldier
Didn't serve in the military but I will kill you quicker than a cobra
The world is in the eye of the beholder,
Since I see everything I guess I'm the majority owner
Hotter than the solar corona
I'm the Coach, MVP 6th man, GM and majority owner
Meaning I got way more than just one skill
I stay getting higher than a Himalayan hill Might catch me pop a pill,
But I'm all about weed smoking like my backyard grill
Love smoking on something greener than a baseball field
From the ground up watch the evolution of my ascendance
Shining brighter than a comet's tail, steadily searching for forgiveness
Broken promises poured water on a situation that was on fire like a car crash
I guess life had other plans, now I'm over here eating with my squad

Know exactly how to save and spend them bands
I like alot of toys, play video games when Im blowed
Doing shit I want and going places I never been before
I'm all about progress looking past the past
Doing my best to not have anymore regrets
Smoke and drink do my thing like everyone else
Nothing can stop me, if I were you I would spread the word about me
Looking for the stacks of cash on pallets in the vault
Sticking up the game got my lyrical trigger finger to its brain
Taking it hostage till I get paid, man
Don't make pull the trigger on the assault, Too Late

Well Of fire

Pyroclastic flow, sit back relax and enjoy the show
No love for a hoe, Love real Ladies with a passion though
Cause they know I got the flow
Super fast fly past throwing money like I'm throwing an elbow
Shows you can catch me selling out, Im winning dont make me shell it out
Hand grenades and switchblades, now the competitions bailing out
Fire straight from the belly, if you think you ready then come on and try and test me
End up like freshly sliced meat from the deli
Fire straight from the dragon's belly
My pen is radioactive, all my ladies are attractive
Do this all day pimpin I don't need no practice
Walk a mile in my shoes, pay the toll pay your dues
Your fett will end up bruised, I know how this ends you loose
Well of fire, like an oil rig on fire, doin lyrical laps while yall punks get tired
My stamp is brand new while yall date close to expired
New hire and yall close to being fired, double tread on my run flat tires
Not in it for the fame, Everybody say that, but they dont got the game
I'm futuristic PS6, none of yall niggas can fuck with this
Don't get it twisted please pay close attention,
Not once did I mention the fact that I got henchmen
Got goons on the squad we don't need bodyguards
Got heavenly fire, all white attire
Straight from GOD is where all my power comes from

What You Want Me To say

What you want me to say?
Im airing out my heart,trying to say everything
To let you know that I don't want to part
I didn't believe in love at first sight,Until I set eyes on You
I wait for the night I can make love to you
Your my every wish, my every dream come true
I would love to spend the rest of my life with you
Every time i touch you I get a rush
Everytime you touch me you can't get enough
I stay ready, like a suitcase overstuffed
Really can't get enough of your sticky stuff
Got my tongue sprung but I'm still eating you out
You saying that you miss me, but out the bed your a mystery
So I guess I need to be silence and secrecy
About my pimpery, and the 5 P's on my CHI shit
On my cold heart, man fuck a bitch
I been trying to tell this bitch but she not with this shit
So Imma move on like the wind
Fingers burnt accused I smoke to much alone
Drink like I'm at the bar, stay up late like the Morning Star
Cast shadows wide and far
Eating dinner inside of castle walls
Money over flowing like Niagara Falls
Got enough charm to knock down a Nun's walls
But I don't want to corrupt the innocent
I try my best to be what the world needs me to be
Because malevolence is a big part of me
But I show benevolence, because that's best way to be

What's Good

Her I stand before the world, with open hands, a mouth full of pearls
Wisdom in every sentence Knowledge in abundance
Understanding about everything, when I was younger I prayed for that
Took some time for me to get here, and now that I've arrived
I can't tell you how good it feels
When your dreams finally come to life
Outside of these pages have to watch out for the cages
Avoid ignorant situations
Living the same except I got way more cash
Still smoking like explosions over Baghdad
Spent a lot of years toking, nothing new but the cash
Been the same since day 1, only difference now we having way more fun
Ain't gotta look over my shoulder when I'm playing ball is the only time I run
Butli do keep a legal chopper in the hoster, Burn you with the toaster
Just in case the situation dictates won't hesitate to send hot ones your way
But I'm all about living good, pooping bottles smoking on some purple good
Riding through the old hood, CHITOWN What's Good?

During my life I have known Love, in its bittersweet form and in its purest.
I can speak on the things that I know best, because I have experience.
Regrets are some of the worst forms of punishment, because there's always the what ifs
Rolling around in your subconscious and heart.

Time itself is a big what if, that we go through daily. The choices we make that affect others That ultimately leads to the experiences we have. Sometimes those choices are taken out of Our hands and we just have to deal with the consequences as best we can.

To be honest this is an amalgamation of all of the relationships I've had during my lifetime. No one situation has led me to write this but all of my past went into the making of this. Years of being alone and loving and trying my best to understand and give my all to some who Were definitely worth time and attention, and obviously some not so worthy.

This project also is a voice for All People. Not everyone has the ability to write fluently and Coherently. I chose this avenue to speak on all the things that I have experienced, not just one specific situation. It would be easy to blame one but it's a lifetime of broken dreams and promises that have shaped the words of my work.

Anyone that has known love in all of its forms knows exactly of what I speak.
From the first Love of my life till the last I owe you all an apology. Not for my words in this work But for not being able to be what I could have been.

Due to having failed relationships in the past I was able to pull out of myself all of the jagged pieces that have caused me so much pain over the years,and begin my healing process. Never be fooled to think that pain is not real, that loneliness does not exist. It is an existential part of who we are as Men and Women. Makes you care even when you know you shouldn't, Makes you doubt your own self worth at times.I guess that's why they call it the blues.

Having said that, I know even in these wicked and tiresome days that there are still good hearts left in this world, that's why GOD hasn't come down and destroyed everything yet. I walk in the knowledge of my failures but I also know that everything truly does happen for a reason. One can’t blame a vase for breaking, a force moved upon the vase to cause it to break.

My desire to reach the highest levels of self awareness and spiritual balance include having a pure true love in my heart, to take away all of the old residual pains from the past. This I know would help me to vibrate at my highest levels and bring purity and peace to my life.

Love is truly one of, if not the greatest of all emotions, and when its pure and its righteous It transforms everything inside of you and breaks the cycle of stagnation and hate that exists in the world. We as a people have everything we need in each other to help boost each other to levels previously unknown

A lonely man or woman does not often have the ability to see beyond their pain. And instead of trying to look forward, we fall deeper still into the stagnation of our past traumas, often turning to drink or drugs to make us feel stronger or to help us to forget the past, not really knowing that we are reliving the traumas that we have experienced when we take that drink or smoke that weed or pop that pill. Reliving those moments as we try to get away from all of the brokenness and traumas.

Far from helping, unfortunately these are the triggers that create the habits that we carry with us daily. Pure emotion can cleanse all of this. We all as humans really do need partners in life whether we want to admit it or not. The hardest thing to admit is that we need others. A rich man or woman still needs something to spend their money on, even if it's an investment.

Key word being needs. Money is not an emotion and can never be a substitute for one. Money creates separation and division, and jealousy between those that have and those that don't. While love motivates one to change their lives to allow the best of themselves to be shown to the world through the Union that is created with someone that they truly love.

Don't get me wrong, I smoke my weed and drink and roll on a pill from time to time just like anybody else. I just know that I use that as a substitute for feeling my best. I think I'm done with all of the excuses for why I am the way I am. Knowing that my Heart Chakra has been closed for so long has made me unbalanced in my life, and it's hard to look past any of the things that caused it to be. Falling for the careless whispers of those that don't truly know how to love has damaged me but I know that my heart is not beyond repair though. Not just my heart but all of us that have had the misfortune of experiencing the dreaded broken heart. It's real and it can last a lifetime if you don't break the cycle!

So to my Brothers and Sisters I say to you Heal your heart so that your energy can flow properly! Be careful of all of the pharmaceuticals ingested and love as hard and as purely as you can.

www.ingramcontent.com/pod-product-compliance
Lightning Source LLC
LaVergne TN
LVHW082252150826
845677LV00009B/1605
9798754511477